What Are They Saying About Unbelief?

Michael Paul Gallagher, SJ

PAULIST PRESS
New York/Mahwah, NJ

Library of Congress Cataloging-in-Publication Data

Gallagher, Michael Paul.
    What are they saying about unbelief? / Michael Paul Gallagher.
      p.   cm.
    Includes bibliographical references.
    ISBN 0-8091-3596-5 (alk. paper)
    1. Catholic Church and atheism—History—20th century. 2. Skepticism—Controversial literature. 3. Atheism—Controversial literature. 4. Catholic Church—Doctrines—History—20th century. I. Title.
BX1397.G35   1995   95-17431
261.2′1—dc20   CIP

Published by Paulist Press
997 Macarthur Boulevard
Mahwah, New Jersey 07430

Printed and bound in the
United States of America

Contents

Introduction: From "Atheism" to "Cultural Unbelief"

"For the first time in the history of the church, a Council is meeting in an age of atheism." That remark from a French bishop during the Second Vatican Council captures the urgency with which this theme exploded into theology during the 1960s. For some decades previously, atheism had been a concern in French Catholic thinking, but the period during and immediately after the council saw it become a major topic for theologians internationally.

Interestingly, it was not the council itself that first gave birth to a new approach to atheism. Pope Paul VI, elected during the years of the council, undertook several personal initiatives toward putting this issue on the council's agenda. He also represented a new wavelength of response to this reality. Three decades later, it can be hard to realize the novelty of his stance, but it was a breakthrough in church history when his first encyclical, *Ecclesiam Suam,* not only described atheism as "the most serious problem of our time" but went on to call for research into the causes of atheism and into why people are "troubled and deny the existence of God." Taking a further and more daring step, the pope recognized the possible moral authenticity of atheists as people "endowed with breadth of mind, and impatient with the mediocrity and self-seeking which contaminate so many areas of human society today."[1]

Thus the new pope spurred the council to take up the issue of atheism with more urgency. Up to then, in the first two sessions, the topic had received little attention. But this papal document of 1964 went well beyond the predictable note of condemnation about the oppression of religion under communist regimes and inaugurated a new age of dialogue. Not for nothing has *Ecclesiam Suam* often been called the "magna carta" of dialogue in the Catholic Church. One of the sections here will examine how in fact the Vatican Council responded to that papal push. In pastoral terms what was new was the non-judgmental tone and the commitment to enter into a new adventure of listening and even learning from unbelievers.

Moreover, what the church *does* is as much theology as what its leaders or experts *say*, and in this respect Pope Paul's approach was institutionalized in a novel way by his setting up a Secretariat for Non-Believers in April 1965. This office of the Vatican went through periods of different focus. In its first decade it concentrated on dialogue itself and then on the phenomenon of secularization. In 1978 it published a major set of essays on religious indifference. During the 1980s and early 1990s it worked on a series of research issues with an increasingly pastoral thrust: science and faith (1981), secular ethics (1983), the new situation of unbelief (1985), ideologies and contemporary mentalities (1988), and Christian faith and the search for happiness (1991). In 1988 it changed its name to the Pontifical Council for Dialogue with Non-Believers, but a more radical change came more recently. Indeed it could be said to symbolize the radically altered situation concerning unbelief when Pope John Paul II, in May 1993, issued a decree merging this council with the Pontifical Council of Culture. The disappearance of "non-believers" from the title was significant: through the years the expression had often been a source of unease, and in recent times dialogue with non-believers in the strict sense had become less and less possible. The pope's instructions to this restructured Pontifical Council of Culture spoke of reflecting on unbelief and religious indifference as part of the "dialogue between faith and cultures." He still encouraged "dialogue with those who do not believe in God" whenever they are open to such an initiative, but the main accent now falls on an "encounter with non-believers in the privileged area of culture."[2]

More Images Than Ideas

This shift of emphasis was a clear recognition of how the dominant form of unbelief today is quite different from the 1960s. Indeed the previous year, in April 1992, Cardinal Paul Poupard, then president of both pontifical councils (Dialogue with Non-Believers and Culture, and now president of the united new body), had given a lecture at Seton Hall University, entitled "Dialogue after the Collapse of Communism." There he emphasized the rapidly changing context for dialogue and seemed to foresee a major shift of agenda:

> It can now become a dialogue free from the prisons of ideology and therefore a dialogue free to explore fundamental spiritual values in a new way. It will be in a new sense a dialogue of faith....
> In this situation of spiritual vulnerability, the need for dialogue has not disappeared. But it will be a dialogue with a different accent....
> It is a pastoral dialogue that reflects on culture in order to serve faith. In this new situation, this dialogue needs to become a spiritual skill of listening in order to proclaim anew the treasure of our Christian truth. [3]

What had changed that led, in a sense, to dropping the title "Dialogue with Non-Believers"? To tackle this question leads us to describe some of the key shifts surrounding faith in contemporary society, and therefore offers a good way of entry into the argument of these pages. Not only had Soviet communism as an atheist system fallen from power, but the whole issue of non-belief has become less linked with pure ideas or imposed ideologies. Instead it is seen as more connected with cultures. Few people live by ideas. Most people, whether believers or non-believers, are more influenced by the images that surround them in their societies and that shape the horizon of their hopes. In this changing context, theological discourse has gradually come to avoid the term "atheism" and to speak rather of "unbelief" or "non-belief." Even this altered vocabulary points to a different agenda—not an "ism" but rather a whole complex of influences in contemporary "mindsets and heartsets" as Peter Steele, an Australian priest-poet, has put it.

The typical tone has moved from a definite and sometimes militant denial of God to a more vague distance from religious faith. Some commentators describe this as the transition from the "modern," with its trust in reason and technology, to the "post-modern," with its skepticism about large humanist claims and its corresponding mood of unease over meanings and values. If the word "atheism" tended to suggest a concrete decision, or a deliberate stance that rejects God, the newer term "unbelief" evokes less clarity and more confusion and doubt. Religious faith is not so much denied as sensed to be unreal. Therefore religious indifference, sometimes allied to a non-dogmatic agnosticism, seems to be the commonest form of unbelief now in North America at present. It is usually interpreted as a by-product of secularized life-styles, even as a "culture of lived atheism."[4] With such a "culture of disbelief," God becomes a "hobby" and this marginalized religion is thus robbed of social seriousness.[5] Certainly, in countries as different as the United States and India, older-style atheists continue to exist, to form associations, and to publish books and journals.[6] But this kind of thought-out negation of the existence of God is much less typical than before: the dominant form of unbelief today is usually a passive product of cultural forces.

God Missing But Not Missed

Even if the tone of contemporary culture has shifted con-siderably and if hard-line atheism has become rare, lack of faith remains a crucial challenge for theology and for the church. This truth and this urgency can be found in three quite independent statements made by theologians in the early 1990s. The first is from the French Dominican writer Jean-Pierre Jossua and the second from a Spanish-Catalan Jesuit, Josep Vives. The third is from a report of the "Mission de France," a group of priests with long experience of working in areas of massive secularization.

> The number one problem which theologians have to confront is that of unbelief, whether argued or lived, and of an indifference and absence of desire toward what to me is most alive and precious: the gospel, the figure of Jesus, the nearness of God.... If we only evoke spiritual experiences, even the deepest or most decisive on a human level, it does not insure that the question of God is posed, and still less does it guarantee that the gospel is accepted with the risk of faith that it entails.[7]

> If the old forms of atheism and agnosticism are now out of date, it is clear that one cannot yet proclaim the reflourishing of theism. What more truly characterizes the present moment is that the question of God remains something irrelevant, or even non-existent for the great majority of people. "God is missing but is not missed." This is a genuinely new situation, which never existed before in the world.[8]

> The novelty of our time is that young people are now born outside any church horizon and are in no way concerned with the church. One has also moved from people who fought against God and God's place in the world of images and ideas to others for whom the question has simply become of no interest.... On the other hand an a-religious universe does not necessarily imply remaining a stranger to God. Not only have we the faith-conviction that God is present to every person, including those in an a-religious world, but we do not set aside the idea that people can be present to God in such a world.[9]

That Mission de France report goes on to describe the religious culture of now as one of both uncertainty and waiting, where commitment is the best bridge between believers and unbelievers.

These contemporary comments seem to have a shared emphasis: that unbelief now has become for many an inherited confusion, a distance from roots, a cultural by-product, an undramatic limbo of indifference. Moreover, this religious vacuum is part of a larger unease and uncertainty about values, about institutions, about the very possibility of finding livable meanings. Such a contemporary sense of absence of faith, and the foreignness of its language, is captured in a powerful satiric poem by James McAuley, who evokes a whole generation of the religiously "disinherited":

> Who do not think or dream, deny or doubt,
> But simply don't know what it's all about.[10]

Nevertheless, in this changed setting of the 1990s, the basic option for dialogue with non-believers has remained—even though it also has inevitably changed in tone. A recent and public example of this openness to dialogue came in some remarks of Pope John Paul II about Mikhail Gorbachev. The ex-president of the Soviet Union had published an article (in March 1992) in which he spoke of a "spiritual understanding between us" and how recent changes "in eastern Europe would not have been possible without the presence of this pope." Commenting on this essay, the pope himself described Gorbachev as "a man of principles, spiritually very rich," and added: "He does not call himself a believer, but with me, I remember, he spoke of the great importance which he attributed to prayer, to the inner dimension."[11]

Even the coincidence that each described the other as "spiritual" is an indicator of a major shift of wavelength. It would have been impossible for one of the communist leaders or one of the popes of the first half of this century to use such language about one another. Equally it is a symbol of a shift within theological reflection on unbelief—that it is increasingly seen in non-doctrinal terms as an existential issue involving the spiritual horizon of each person and indeed of each culture.

This book will seek to do justice to various approaches to unbelief over the last few decades. But even from the outset it should be clear that we are talking about the fate of faith under the pressure of modernity—and modernity has many faces. It is impossible to separate theology concerning unbelief from theology concerning faith today. Indeed the very existence of various forms of atheism has proved not only a challenge but a purification for theology of faith.

Not only has modernity many faces: so also has "unbelief" or "atheism." At its deepest it is a total refusal of God, not just with the mind but with one's existence. Usually, however, when people speak of atheism or non-belief, they do not mean this radical version of "fundamental sin" as Karl Rahner called it. Instead they are thinking of people who interpret their existence without reference to God, or who either reject or avoid religious faith and its usual embodiments. In the course of these chapters, we shall examine the sheer variety of positions intended by the phenomenon of "unbelief."

In selecting theologians to explore and summarize here, preference has been given to the pastoral approach: How can the believer understand and respond to an unbeliever friend? Such a question and such a desire are on the lips of many people today, whether they be theologians or pastors, parents or teachers, or just ordinary believers who care about their faith and care about their friends.

Diversity of Horizons

Some comment is necessary about what these pages will not seek to cover. In such a vast field some selection was necessary, and these chapters limit themselves to some theological and pastoral discussions of unbelief, mainly from a European and North

American perspective. Even the theme of "secularization" will be touched on rarely: many see this as mainly a European phenomenon and less relevant for the United States, where religious adherence has always been "free and voluntary," not mixed up with the ambiguities of a powerful or established church.[12]

From another viewpoint, it can be argued that only the richer world has the luxury of this question of meaning, and that in the situations of massive poverty in the "south" of our planet, atheism means more the practical denial of God in the oppression of people. Although the Latin American situation will receive only brief attention here, issues of secularization have received fresh attention there in recent years, and a symposium in Costa Rica in 1992 summed up the dominant unbelief in these words: "The phenomenon of religious indifference exists mostly in the urban areas, where the majority of Latin Americans now live, and it is especially found among the ruling classes. But through the communication media and other factors, this same mentality is making itself felt in rural areas."[13]

Again, the so-called "New Age" tendency can be interpreted as a subtle and post-modern face of unbelief, because it promotes a soft and even egoist spirituality, shy of Christian revelation, and silent on the cost of commitment. But, like the other horizons just mentioned, that could be a theme for another book. The focus here is to gather what theologians have been saying explicitly about unbelief over recent decades, and to offer some sense of how that debate has developed differently in different countries—as well as how it has changed in tone over the years.

Finally, debate on this issue has been a particularly lively one outside the Anglo-American world, and indeed many of the theologians to be mentioned here have never been translated into English. Therefore this book hopes to offer the English-speaking reader a glimpse of the diversity of this field internationally, and, because of this, individual chapters are often deliberately geographical. Incidentally, where translations do not exist, the English version is my own.

Notes

1. *Ecclesiam Suam*, Pars. 55, 58.
2. *L'Osservatore Romano* (English Weekly Edition), 12 May 1993, p.3.
3. Cardinal Paul Poupard, "Dialogue after the Collapse of Communism," *Atheism and Faith*, XXVII, No 2, 1992, pp. 82, 84, 90.
4. John F. Kavanaugh, *Following Christ in a Consumer Society* (Maryknoll: Orbis Books, 1981), p. 112.
5. Stephen L. Carter, *The Culture of Disbelief: how American law and politics trivialize religious devotion* (New York: Harper Collins, 1993), p. 16.
6. Prometheus Books, a publishing house based in Buffalo, New York, specializes in atheist books and has just celebrated twenty–five years of its existence. It is also associated with such periodicals as *Free Inquiry* and *Skeptical Inquirer*. A recent issue of *International Humanist News* (March 1994) listed nearly one hundred journals worldwide that promote secularist philosophy. These include *The Freethinker* and *Humanist News* in England.
7. Jean–Pierre Jossua, "Le Congrès 1990 de *Concilium,*" *Recherches des Sciences Religieuses* (LXXIX, 1991), p. 27.
8. Josep Vives, "Dios en el crepusculo del siglo XX," *Razón y Fe*, Mayo 1991, p. 468.
9. "Comment dire Dieu à l'homme d'aujourd'hui?" *Lettre aux Communautés de la Mission de France*, No. 158, janvier–février 1993, pp. 18–30.
10. James McCauley, "A Letter to John Dryden," in *Anthology of Australian Religious Poetry*, ed. Les Murray (North Blackburn: Collins Dove, 1991), p. 168.
11. *La Stampa* (Italian newspaper), 3 March and 10 March 1992.
12. See Robert Kress, "Religiously Indifferent or Religiously Different," *Kerygma* (Ottawa: vol. 24, 1990), pp. 143–159. Quotation from p. 154.
13. "El indiferentismo y el sincretismo religiosos; Desafios e prop-uestas pastorales para la nueva evangelizacion en America Latina," *Atheism and Faith*, XXVII (1992), pp. 41–49. Quotation from p. 41.

A Note on Terminology

The various words that cover the phenomenon of "unbelief" do not have any fixed usage or meaning. But perhaps some clarity is possible.

Atheism: outright denial of the existence of God, often implying a conscious and intellectually grounded choice.

This is sometimes sub-divided into "positive atheism," which militantly combats the very idea of God, and "negative atheism," implying a world-view that insists on the absence of God and the capacity of living happily without any religious dimension.

Unbelief or *Non–Belief*: "softer" terms meaning the absence or rejection of religious faith, or else attitudes to life which do not include any transcendent dimension.

Practical Atheism or *Practical Unbelief*: the emphasis here is on the lived dimension rather than the conceptual; consumerist life-styles, for instance, can block the possibility of faith. A merely "nominal Christian" could be a "practical atheist."

Systematic Atheism: the political imposing of godless philoso-phies of life in a society. A classic example would be the Marxist

11

attempt to propagate a materialist world–view through education and the prohibition of religious organizations.

Agnosticism: a word first used by T.H. Huxley in 1869 to signify that one does not know and cannot know whether God exists: hence religious truth can neither be affirmed or denied.

Indifference: a psychological attitude of disinterest in God or faith, rather than an intellectual stance. It is also used where church embodiments of religion and/or the very question of God seem irrelevant or unreal.

Doubt: being in two minds, vacillation, non-decision, caught between contrary and conflicting judgments over the reality of God.

Secular Humanism: the assertion that science and human values are sufficient to make sense of life, and indeed that to believe in God is an escape from human responsibility and dignity.

Secularism and *Secularization*: not the same thing. The first is a doctrine that denies any validity to the religious dimension, especially in the public sphere. The second is, in theory, an historically neutral process whereby religious institutions let go of social control and encourage the genuine autonomy of human activities. But although this process can liberate and purify faith, it is often ambiguous in practice, and so "secularization" has come to mean a retreat of faith into the private realm, a diminishing of Christian belonging, and a decline of religious values in society. In short, secularization slides easily toward secularism.

1
A Chapter of Church History

New Option for Sympathy

The moment of church history represented by the evolution of attitudes toward atheism during Vatican II is a significant one. The debates on this topic during the council revealed some inevitable tensions between models of theology, of church, even of God. It represented a Catholic version of the contrast of approach found between Barth and Tillich. Where Barth stressed the differentness of faith and the role of revelation as absolute judgment on the world, Tillich was much more inclined to an ascending theology for today, in the sense of starting from human realities and, in their light, trying to make sense of revelation. To choose the first is to base oneself in the undeniable transcendence of God's truth but at the risk of non-relevance and of speaking a language remote from history now. To choose the second is to opt for pastoral communication as crucial and, like St. Paul in Athens, to seek to enter by the door of the culture surrounding one's audience. The first is the stance of a mainly dogmatic theology, the second of a mainly pastoral theology.

It is significant that the Vatican II stance on atheism represented a victory for the pastoral emphasis, and this in spite of the fact that the more "conservative" school had been particularly entrenched in the years preceding the council. It was typical of this ruling

mentality that the only references to atheism in the documents
prepared in advance for the council dealt with it from the perspective of an embattled and, one might say, cold war perspective
within religion. These texts approached atheism from four rather
limited perspectives: from the point of view of preservation of
faith, or as needing a reaffirmation of the proofs of the existence of
God, or in terms of condemnation of errors, or under the heading
of the menace of communist atheism. As the council progressed,
this method was found to be not so much untrue as inadequate to a
quite new pastoral situation in the modern world. The problem of
God came to be viewed as not only one of truth or error, but rather
of how a convergence of historical factors caused an eclipse of the
sense of God for many people today. In short, the council fathers
discovered gradually that they had to face not simply a
philosophical or ideological crisis of faith, but a much more
profound shift in culture. A new starting point was needed and it
was eventually found in humanity itself, in terms of what came to
be officially called "Christian anthropology."

How did the council move from the rigid stance of the
proposed documents to the first extended and largely pastoral
statement on atheism in conciliar history? How did the council
arrive at what was described, at its close, by Pope Paul VI as an
"immense sympathy" instead of a spirit of "struggle" or of
condemnation? The process of that conversion, as witnessed in
the decisions concerning atheism, is a symbolic miniature of a
more general shift within the Church: from ghetto to listening,
from anathema to dialogue, from abstract certainties to an
urgency about renewal of the language of faith. In this light, some
summary is offered of the debates that led to that change of tone
and heart. Even though the final statements on atheism (in
sections 19 to 21 of *Gaudium et Spes*) might seem slight—like a
short essay of two thousands words—its novelty is appreciated
best with some knowledge of the drama of the discussions that
underlie its every sentence. This complex story has been told by
various authors. Here only a skeleton summary will be offered.[1]

It was not until the third year of the council in 1964 that the issue of atheism came into full focus, spurred on by the positive stance taken by Paul VI in his first encyclical, *Ecclesiam Suam*, published a month before the third session began—and its historical importance has been mentioned already in the Introduction of this book. This papal statement had a crucial role in bringing the issue to the forefront of attention, but the discussion itself went through various stages of development. In his analysis of the 1964 or first of the two conciliar debates on atheism, Paul Ladrière noted two polarities: those who saw injustice and mediocre Christian living as sources of unbelief were also inclined to downplay its philosophical aspects and to acknowledge positive moral values in unbelievers.[2] On the other side were those who tended both to identify atheism with communism and to stress the intellectual dangers of this phenomenon. But the main progress made at this stage was an agreement that the topic should be seriously treated and that it needed to be approached as a human reality of today. Thus a special sub-committee was appointed to draft a new statement, and this became known as the Ariccia text—from the meeting place of the working party.

This new text, prepared for the 1965 or final session of the council, began as follows: "Unfortunately, many of our contemporaries have no idea, or no right idea, of humanity's intimate and vital relationship with God."[3] Starting from the existential reality that all persons remain "an unanswerable question" for themselves, the draft went on to list various forms of unbelief: exaggerated humanism, the stifling of the question of faith through indifference, distorted images of God, and alienation from religion due to the fault of believers themselves. This Ariccia document also included a longer passage tone concerning forms of "systematic denial of God's existence."[4] Even though it did not name communism, it was obvious that this was an attempt to touch on this version of atheism without the older language of condemnation.

As it happens, even this Ariccia text was fairly severely criticized and altered as a result of the 1965 debate. Since he had recently been named president of the new Secretariat for Non-Believers, the speech of Cardinal Franz König of Vienna was especially influential. He complained that "nothing is found on the remedies to be sought and on how the church should act," and he called for a deeper treatment of the roots of atheism.[5] Cardinal Seper of Zagreb advocated greater self-critique by believers: "a partial responsibility of this modern atheism rests with those Christians" who obstinately defend the social status quo "in the name of God."[6] In fact both cardinals were appointed to head a new sub-commission which would shape the final statement to be included in *Gaudium et Spes*.

Although in previous sessions many bishops from eastern Europe had called for a renewed condemnation of communism, this emphasis now gave way to a more explicitly pastoral one. A speech by Archbishop Wojtyla, the future pope, proved influential in this respect. In 1964 he had warned that this section needed to avoid ecclesiastical language; if it did not, it would fall into soliloquy, the opposite of dialogue. Now he offered a distinction "between atheism which arises from personal conviction and that which makes use of unjust means." In his view this *pastoral* constitution should not deal with the political issue, which was more suited to the document on religious freedom, and instead it should treat unbelief as "an interior state of the human person…a problem of soul, mind and heart."[7]

Other speeches in this debate stressed the link between atheism and injustice. Thus Cardinal Maximos Saigh of Antioch argued that "the true socialism is Christianity" and that if we had lived it more fully, "the world would have been spared atheistic communism."[8] Bishop Pildáin y Zapiáin proposed that "liberal capitalism" was also a source of injustice and that its inequalities should be solemnly condemned.[9] Others spoke of the danger of religion as a cause of alienation and of dialogue with unbelievers as potentially purifying for the faith of the believer. All in all this

1965 debate was remarkably open and it prepared the way for the positive and pastoral tone of the *Gaudium et Spes* text.

Strengths and Weaknesses

There is no need to analyze the relevant paragraphs here. Readers of this book will have easy access to the document. Instead this section can close with a summary of some of the theological commentary on this first-ever conciliar statement on atheism.

The text has been criticized from at least four different angles.

(1) Some complained about its neglect of the perspective of revelation. Karl Barth questioned whether it is so "certain that dialogue with the world is to be placed ahead of proclamation to the world."[10] This is to ask for a significantly different approach to that chosen by the council, and indeed it is a direction that has gained ground inside Catholicism within the last decade or so. But the stance of the council was quite deliberate: in the words of Paul Ladrière, the "drafters of the text did not believe it possible to address themselves to atheists directly in the name of Judeo-Christian revelation."[11]

(2) However, the same Ladrière pointed to different weaknesses: he discerned a latent "persistence of ecclesiocentrism." By this he meant that the church tended almost to identify itself with faith, and hence to merge atheism as an anti-religious reaction with atheism as a denial of God.[12]

(3) In a somewhat similar vein, he would fault the council for not breaking more firmly with an older tradition of natural theology: although it embraced a more phenomenological and personalist language, it still assumed that God is accessible to reason and conscience by virtue of human nature. Hence the text can be accused of straddling two languages—perhaps a necessary doubleness in this whole question of human avenues to God.[13]

(4) Finally, *Gaudium et Spes* on atheism has been criticized for its lack of reference to "negative theology." Even though an early

paragraph (*GS* 7) admits that secularism can offer a healthy purification of religion, the relevance of "apophatic" theology for questions of unbelief is not expressed by the council. This ancient tradition would insist that the human language will always remain incapable of doing justice to the mystery of God. In this century its adherents would counter the danger of defending a merely deist God with a sense of how the darkness found in the mystics is not unlike the experiences of some anguished atheists.[14]

Equally, one can pick out four positive aspects that have been praised in these paragraphs of the council.

(1) André Charron notes the courage to abandon a merely "objectivist" analysis of ideas for a more "humanist" perspective, involving "inductive method." In this way the question of unbelief is located within the "problem of humanity," and the implicit theological method has shifted from a rationalist rejection of error to an existential reading of human realities of today's culture.[15]

(2) Johann Figl has noted a parallel shift away from "political theology" toward "religious anthropology": the council stopped identifying atheism almost exclusively with communism, separated that issue by placing it under religious freedom, and hence was free to adapt a more personalist and spiritual approach to unbelief.[16]

(3) In terms of moral theology, Karl Rahner has highlighted the significant silence of the council on the previously prevailing assumption that atheism is usually sinful. Indeed, the council seems to affirm the opposite, that it is possible to profess explicit atheism throughout a lifetime without this being proof of moral guilt, and without (as we shall see shortly) thereby making salvation unattainable.[17]

(4) The short section on atheism can also be praised as a minor masterpiece of balance, in particular for the way it achieves a synthesis of three elements: a new awareness of the complexity of atheism, an attitude of sympathy toward unbelievers, and an

historically new invitation to dialogue between believers and unbelievers. Taken together these three developments spell the end of any mere hostility of the church toward those who do not believe in God. All three options are rooted in a sense of humility, which confesses the role of impoverished religious living in giving rise to unbelief, and at the same time they show courage in embracing a new historical consciousness, in acknowledging the radically changed context for faith presented by contemporary culture.

New Optimism About Salvation

Before closing this chapter on Vatican II, some brief mention should be made of its stance on a traditional theological question—the salvation of the unbeliever. On three occasions the texts of the council touch on this issue, and they add up to a major development in official Catholic teaching. The three places are *Lumen Gentium* 16, *Gaudium et Spes* 22, and *Ad Gentes* 7. Once again it seems unnecessary to give extensive quotations here. What emerges is that it is not essential to have an explicit faith in God in order to belong within the possibility of salvation. It is important, however, to view the three statements together as a unity. On its own, the *Lumen Gentium* paragraph was accused by Joseph Ratzinger of bordering on Pelagianism by placing too much emphasis on human striving, or the effort of being faithful to one's conscience.[18] But with *Gaudium et Spes* the emphasis is given to God's salvific action as universal even if hidden—"in some way known to God" (*modo Deo cognito*). The Decree on the Church's Missionary Activity makes one significant addition to this accumulating understanding. It uses the word "faith" in such a way as to suggest a distinction between it and the "explicit knowledge of God" spoken of in *Lumen Gentium*: in ways known to God (*viis sibi notis*), those who do not know the gospel can be led to that faith without which salvation is impossible (cf. Heb 11:6). In short, the council affirms the possibility of a faith that need not be explicit, and furthermore holds that this implicit faith is a ground for optimism concerning the potential salvation of the unbeliever.

A quarter of a century after Vatican Council II, Pope John Paul II's encyclical *Redemptoris Missio* offered an even stronger summary statement of the church's position on this question. Referring back to the *Gaudium et Spes* statement, it developed the stance as follows with an additional focus on the question of church belonging:

> The universality of salvation means that it is granted not only to those who explicitly believe in Christ and have entered the church. Since salvation is offered to all, it must be made concretely available to all. But it is clear that today, as in the past, many people do not have an opportunity to come to know or accept the gospel revelation or to enter the church. The social and cultural conditions in which they live do not permit this, and frequently they have been brought up in other religious traditions. For such people salvation in Christ is accessible by virtue of a grace which, while having a mysterious relationship to the church, does not make them formally part of the church but enlightens them in a way which is accommodated to their spiritual and material situation. This grace comes from Christ; it is the result of his sacrifice and is communicated by the Holy Spirit. It enables each person to attain salvation through his or her free cooperation.[19]

This text offers a new balance between the gift of God and the response of human freedom, between the culturally and historically conditioned situations that leave many people unable to reach explicit faith and a very positive view of the mystery of salvation as universally available.

Notes

1. Later in this chapter, various articles by Paul Ladrière will be cited. In addition one may mention: M.P. Gallagher, "The Birth of a

New Ecumenism: Attitudes to Atheism in Vatican I," *Milltown Studies* (Dublin), No. 6, 1980, pp. 1-35, and Johann Figl, *Atheismus als theologisches Problem* (Mainz: Mattias-Grüneward-Verlag, 1977) pp. 31-81.

2. Paul Ladrière,"L'Athéisme au Vatican II," *Social Compass*, XXIV (1977), pp. 347-391, esp. p. 363.

3. *Acta Synodalia Sacrosancti Concilii Oecumenici Vaticani II* (Vatican City, 1970 ff.), Vol. IV, Part 1, 446.

4. P. 447.

5. *Acta*, Vol. II, Part 2, 454.

6. P. 436.

7. P. 662.

8. P. 453.

9. P. 489.

10. Karl Barth, *Ad Limina Apostolorum: An Appraisal of Vatican II* (Richmond: John Knox Press, 1968), p. 27.

11. Paul Ladrière, "Vatican II et la Non-Croyance," in *2000 Ans de Christianisme*, ed. J. Puyo (Paris, 1976), Volume 10, p. 184.

12. Ladrière, as in note 2, pp. 380-381.

13. Paul Ladrière, "L'Athéisme au Concile Vatican II," *Archives de Sociologie des Religions*, XXXI, (1971), pp. 53-84.

14. Ladrière, 1971 article, p. 78.

15. André Charron, *Les Catholiques face à l'athéisme contemporain* (Montreal: Fides, 1973), pp. 248-256.

16. Figl, pp. 51, 66.

17. Karl Rahner, "Atheism and Implicit Christianity," in *Theological Investigations* (London: Darton, Longman & Todd, 1972), p. 147.

18. Joseph Ratzinger, "The Dignity of the Human Person," in *Commentary on the Documents of Vatican II*, ed. H. Vorgrimler (New York: Herder and Herder, 1969), Vol. V, p. 162.

19. *Redemptoris Missio* (1990), Par. 10.

2
Pioneering Thinker: De Lubac

God as an Enemy of Human Freedom

In 1945 a work appeared in France that was to become a classic in this whole area, and indeed its author had a major influence on the Second Vatican Council. Henri de Lubac's *The Drama of Atheistic Humanism* at first glance seems to be a study of nineteenth century thinkers such as Feuerbach, Nietzsche, and Comte, but it is not simply a history of philosophy. He deals with three types of atheism: the Marxist, the positivist and the Nietzschean. But by highlighting the imaginative dimension of the debate on faith, as exemplified in the fiction of Dostoevsky, de Lubac shows his basic sense of atheism as lived "drama," as a tragically mistaken choice, and not simply a matter of ideas. He also sees this modern denial of God as being asserted in the name of human liberation; as such it could more precisely be called *anti*theism or even *anti*–Christianity.

These negations have two pillars: they are grounded in resentment against the ills and illusions of religion and, positively, they want to construct an alternative human freedom. This line of thinkers saw God only as an obstacle to human dignity. And yet they recognized spiritual needs in people. Everyone knows of Marx's view of religion as the "opium of the people," but in context that phrase is not just an arrogant dismissal. It is preceded by a recognition that "religion is the sigh of the creature overwhelmed by unhappiness, the soul of a world that has no heart." De Lubac's reading of this school of thinkers was both sympathetic and critical, and yet ultimately theological.

Faced with this phenomenon, what were some of the pioneering assumptions of de Lubac? Today they may seem obvious—because they have influenced the mainstream of theology for decades now—but they were not so commonplace when he first enunciated them. He also broke new ground with his emphasis on atheism as a spiritual and cultural phenomenon rather than as a narrowly intellectual crisis. In this way he is one of the founding fathers of modern dialogue with non-believers.

A key stance of de Lubac is found in the opening pages of *The Drama of Atheistic Humanism*, when he uses his knowledge of the fathers to situate and set an agenda for discussing modern atheism. In an eloquent passage he evokes the freshness and "radiant newness" felt in Christ in the early centuries. "No more blind hazard! No more *Fate*! Transcendent God, God the friend of all, revealed in Jesus, opened for all a way which nothing would ever bar again."[1] In contrast with this sense of joy, he discerns a sadness and disappointment at the root of modern atheism, where the humanist version of rejection of God goes beyond mere hedonism and becomes instead an assertion of human autonomy. This atheism is not theoretical but existential. De Lubac quotes Nietzsche's statement that "it is our preference that decides against Christianity—not arguments."[2] Pastorally de Lubac's central desire was to find a new language for mystery that would restore a freshness to faith for this disillusioned humanity. He was also convinced that without God, humanism would descend into an anti-humanism. "Lost faith cannot long remain unreplaced";[3] God's place is quickly taken by dangerous idols, addictions that can be personal, social or even political. Dostoevsky was unique in recognizing a contradiction at the heart of such atheism. In de Lubac's words, "man cannot organize the world for himself without God; without God he can only organize the world *against man.* Exclusive humanism is inhuman humanism."[4]

Beyond Mere Rationalism

If this new version of atheism is grounded in a choice against God and in favor of humanity, historically and culturally how did it come about? De Lubac is honest in his critique of religion and of the failures of theology. As early as 1932, in a letter to Blondel, he thanked him for a statement that had served as a spur to reflection in this whole area: "If all too often today people find their lives withdrawn from Christianity, it is perhaps because too often Christianity has got out of touch with the gut-level depths of humanity" (*des viscères de l'homme*).[5] In this respect de Lubac constantly criticized the tendency of older apologetics to be merely defensive, externalist, and narrowly rationalist. Instead, he wanted a cultural and spiritual theology that would examine the situation for faith now and identify the dispositions required for the receiving of revelation. Thus it was typical of his approach to give much of *The Drama of Atheistic Humanism* to evoking the positions of atheism and faith through a contrast between two such passionate writers as Nietzsche and Dostoevsky. We are, he remarked, "relearning, if not the use, at least the understanding of symbols."[6]

Human beings are living paradoxes and mysteries. Theologically the desire for God is natural in that all are drawn toward God whether they know it or not. Therefore if this crucial dimension is stunted, tragedy results. To confront the contemporary crisis of faith, in de Lubac's view, what is needed is not some formula for proving the existence of God: the "taste for God" is in trouble. It is something beyond philosophy. It is "no longer an historical, metaphysical, political or social problem. It is a *spiritual* problem.... The Christian conception of life, Christian spirituality, the inward attitude which, more than any particular act or outward gesture, bespeaks the Christian—that is what is at stake.... Insofar as we have allowed it to be lost, we must rediscover the *spirit* of Christianity. In order to do so we must be plunged once more in its wellsprings."[7]

In short Henri de Lubac's importance lay in setting a new agenda of how theology could approach atheism. He saw little hope in a "dryness" of ideas. He shifted the focus to the more crucial wavelength of human desires and dispositions. He acknowledged the "genius" of an atheist such as Nietzsche. He admired the courage of a Kierkegaard. But his fundamental hope was to revive something of the patristic reverence for mystery, and to evoke the huge loss entailed in modern culture when that dimension seems to disappear. He devoted nearly a third of *The Drama of Atheistic Humanism* to Auguste Comte as summing up the positivist pride of leaving even atheism behind. As Comte himself liked to remark, "Only what is replaced is destroyed."[8] Thus he wanted to establish a firm cult of humanity with a priesthood of the scientists. But de Lubac sees this whole project as dangerously misjudging human nature, ultimately as rather innocent in thinking that such deep questions could be so easily stifled forever.

Unbelief as Tragic Woundedness

In this light, a central de Lubac theme, and one that influenced papal thinking in the decades ahead, was that atheistic humanism was bound to end in bankruptcy. While such a stance might seem arrogant to humanists themselves, it is an essentially theological viewpoint: if God exists and calls humanity into faith and love, then to miss this vision means living within a stunted horizon full of self-contradictions. Indeed this central judgment of his is expressed with a different focus in his later book (never translated into English) *Athéisme et Sens de l'Homme* (1968). Here he ponders the exclusion of transcendence in the analytical world of science, with its absence of "I," and he concludes: "This death-of-God would also be the death of mankind."[9]

The main concern of this later book is to reflect on the insights of Vatican II about atheism, which de Lubac views as the very hinge of *Gaudium et Spes*. One particular fruit that he hopes for from the new alliance, as he calls it, between believers and non-believers is a mutual liberation from "every false image of God and from every idolatry of humanity."[10] But he also sees dangers. While contemporary unbelief is less "aristocratic" than its predecessors, it is in fact more "virulent" in its message that faith has had its day and is now an exhausted form of meaning.[11] Against this dismissiveness, de Lubac identifies the pastoral response of the church in terms of self-critique: one has to combat the "practical atheism" even of believers, which is both a product and a source of the "theoretical atheism" around.[12]

This later book is more aware of the dangers to faith involved for believers who would dialogue with atheism, and in typical fashion de Lubac sees the possible difficulties as more spiritual than intellectual. As regards this "spiritual confrontation," he warns against any excessive bending over backward to justify atheism, or any tendency to secularize the essential language of Christian witness. Equally he is wary of too much talk about "doubt" being part of faith.[13] Certainly the experience of the believer, on a psychological level, entails an inevitable instability, but "to say that there is always an unbeliever within the believer" does not mean that faith itself is composed of unbelief and belief, because faith roots itself in a relationship to the steadiness of the living God.[14]

In this regard de Lubac expresses caution about rushing into "negative theology." It is one thing to recognize the limits of human understanding and language as trying to express the mystery of God. But if this fundamental insight of negative theology is brought into play too soon, it can become the "negation of theology."[15] In his collection of insights translated into English under the title of *The Discovery of God*, de Lubac expressed this with greater force. The wisdom of negative theology is "the 'no' which follows on the 'yes'" and which does not fall into the "hesitations of agnosticism." The danger is that "in a climate of unbelief, negative theology has a fatal tendency to drift toward agnosticism." But for a genuinely negative theology, "silence comes at the end, not at the beginning." [16]

Looking back at his achievement from nearly half a century later, de Lubac's version of unbelief seems dated, but in a significant way. The atheism he had in mind was the committed and even agonized kind, and one that compelled a certain admiration. On this he quoted Dostoevsky to the effect that "perfect atheism is worth more than worldly indifference" and could even be a step on the ladder toward faith.[17] This unbelief that so interested de Lubac is precisely the kind that has decreased in the years since he wrote—as was touched on in the Introduction here. Indeed the culturally conditioned unbelief of this late twentieth century seems out of tune with the three key words of his celebrated title: it lacks drama, it suspects humanism, and even the term "atheism" itself seems too strong for the contemporary scene of absence or rejection of faith. He remains a pioneering theologian concerning atheism, but his perspective belongs very much to the mid-century and to the period of the Second Vatican Council.

Notes

1. *The Drama of Atheistic Humanism* (New York: New American Library, 1963), trans. E. Riley, p. 5.
2. P. 22.
3. P. 158.
4. P. ix.
5. *Mémoire sur l'occasion de mes écrits* (Namur: Culture et Vérité, 1989), p. 189.
6. P. 43.
7. Pp. 62, 72.
8. P. 99.
9. *Athéisme et Sens de l'Homme* (Paris: Cerf, 1968), p. 50.
10. P. 20.

11. P. 32.

12. P. 71.

13. Pp. 72–73, 77.

14. Pp. 78, 80.

15. P. 81.

16. *The Discovery of God* (London: Darton Longman & Todd, 1960), trans. A. Dru, pp. 202, 208, 122.

17. *Drama*, p. 178.

3
Karl Rahner's "Theology of Atheism"

A Pastoral Urgency

In the perspective of the history of ideas, atheism as a philosophical system has always appeared at moments of crisis and transition from one intellectual, cultural and social epoch to another. That shows that it is a crisis phenomenon, the projection of a question disguised as an answer.[1]

There was to be found towards the end of the eighteenth and beginning of the nineteenth centuries a theoretical and practical atheism which really was so unpardonably naive and so culpably superficial as to assert that it knew there is no God.... The case is quite different with troubled atheism [der bekümmerte Atheismus]...alarm at the absence of God from the world...this experience, which imagines that it must interpret itself theoretically as atheism, is a genuine experience of deepest existence (*TI*, III, 390).

An atheism conditioned by today's rationalistic and technological society...is today something that has no precedent in world history.... The vast majority of atheists today in East and West are not people for whom the question of God is really an alarming and agonizing problem (*TI*, XXI, 137, 141).

The focus of Karl Rahner's theology, in spite of all its intellectuality, is basically pastoral and cultural. It remained a constant desire of his, through his long career as a thinker, to make sense of faith for the secular setting of today, and to theologize in ways understandable to inquiring unbelievers. A concern with atheism was an influential and unifying strand in all periods of Rahner's thinking. Has any other major theologian written an article to help believers to ponder the religious situation of unbelievers in their family circle? Has any other theologian tried to write "A Brief Summary of Christian Faith for Unbelievers"?

The widespread unbelief of this century varies from vehemence to simple unsureness, from cool but definite dismissiveness of religion to just disinterest. All these various situations were discussed at various times by Rahner. His awareness of a radically different context for faith underlies his insistence on an anthropological approach within theology: to reach modern unbelievers, in his view, you need to offer a different initial wavelength than scriptural revelation. Therefore he prefers to start from the mystery of existence as experienced in order to move toward a possible threshold of faith. In other words, he always begins "from below," from the quest for meaning and love within every person, and at the core of that adventure of self-transcendence Rahner discerns the mystery of God.

But this existential approach to theology is much more than a pastoral strategy. It is not only an attractive entry to religious issues through humanist perspectives. With his own philosophical background and hermeneutics, people for Rahner are much more than their expressed self-understandings, and this has a special application in the case of atheists or unbelievers. In his view it is a fundamental truth about human life that God is present within people's depth experiences. It is equally an essential truth for him that God is mystery and hence not to be equated with any object or captured in any human concept. God's presence as silent mystery guides each person into trusting their longing to love and be loved, and so it is through reflecting on such key moments when a person reaches out beyond egoism that one can glimpse this invitation and action of God.

Depths of Everyday Experience

This is what is meant by Rahner's transcendental analysis of self-transcendence: transcendental in that it discerns universal fundamentals of the human condition and self-transcending in that each person experiences a whole range of desires to go beyond the little world of self. Where does Rahner see these basics becoming real or existential? Within the ordinary experiences of this world, within the flow of history and within the concrete calls of everyday relationships and commitments.

To read (or write) these sentences is itself an act of self-transcendence—in seeking to understand (or to share an understanding). More broadly, each person harbors a hunger for meaning and for love—even though this can easily be trivialized in modern culture into distraction of all kinds, or else avoided or suppressed in a more deliberate refusal to follow one's conscience. Over the years Rahner changed his interpretation of what lay at the center of modern unbelief: in the 1960s he tended to concentrate on the *concept* of God that was being rejected, whereas by the 1970s he saw the very *question* of God being stifled by the surrounding culture. Thus militant or explicit atheism gave way to a more passive situation of religious indifference—a pervasive secularism that shaped "a single atheistic mentality and way of life" (*TI*, XI, 170). Hence in Rahner's view what is at stake today is not the content of the creed but the very ability to believe.

> A person can, of course, shrug his shoulders and ignore this experience of transcendence.... Most people will do this in a naive way. They live at a distance from themselves in that concrete part of their lives and of the world around them which can be manipulated and controlled...[deciding that] one does well to suppress the question about the meaning of it all (*FCF*, 32-33).

The real argument against Christianity is the experience of life, this experience of darkness. And I have always found that behind the technical arguments leveled by the learned against Christianity…there are always these ultimate experiences of life causing the spirit and the heart to be sombre, tired and despairing (*TI*, V, 5-6).

Living Out One's Freedom

Still more central to Rahner's theological concerns was the fate of a person's deep desire for God. When this orientation (what Rahner calls a transcendental) finds echo in people's freedom (in what Rahner calls the categorial), then they are in touch with the call of grace within them. Whether they name that call God or not (hence Rahner's famous notion of a possibly anonymous response to God—to be discussed in more detail later), they are concretely exercising their liberty and responding to God in all their choosing (which accumulated into what he calls a fundamental option). Thus a person may be unable to name or recognize God on the level of truth but nevertheless can actually be responding to God on the level of decision. Existence as lived is more important for Rahner than any of its interpretations. To ponder this area of self-experience is to appreciate and identify what is deepest in human nature—a capacity to choose to live in truth and in goodness, and a desire to live that way. A recognition of these fundamentals of human experience can also be a crucial step toward faith, toward recognizing the mysterious presence of God at the core of human existence (what Rahner calls the supernatural existential, meaning the universal presence of grace).

In short, in Rahner's theology, God is always present, inescapably so, at the center of each human life. How, then, does unbelief arise? That presence can easily be unrecognizable either because of the divine reticence of such a silent revelation, or because of many cultural changes and pressures today. What is important to note is the Rahnerian shift in the agenda of faith and unbelief—away from the more common emphasis on explicit beliefs, church mediations, conceptual creeds and even from scriptural revelation as central or foundational. Instead he chooses, as part of his pastoral response to unbelief, to search for God more slowly, more tentatively, and starting from human mystery as the gateway to the divine mystery.

In this sense Rahner is doing "depth theology," so to speak, rather like depth psychology: he is interested in the subterranean currents of God's grace and of human response—well beneath the clarity of concepts or statements. In this way he changes the agenda of theology. He is less interested in what believers or unbelievers think or say, or why they think or say it, than in the realm of encounter with mystery happening always at the heart of each existence. Thus a major hope of his theology is to explore the depth-experiences shared by believers and non-believers alike; in this way he seeks to create an existential ecumenism that will undercut inevitable divergences on the level of church belonging or theistic interpretation. If this succeeds, the dialogue will be much deeper than one of ideas alone.

Four Basic Pillars

What are some of the main themes and points of emphasis in Rahner's theology concerning atheism or atheists? With this general approach established, it is possible to list his major ideas fairly briefly and even schematically.

1. *Universal orientation toward God.* If a river were conscious, it would affirm the existence of the ocean toward which it flows; so too all experience of self-transcendence points, even if unconsciously, toward the horizon and goal that is God.

2. *Response on the level of freedom.* We know God implicitly in all the options of life and respond to God without necessarily having conscious religious faith. Therefore ultimately love is a form of faith, and is even more important than explicit faith. God

is encountered in the story of each person and in the drama of history. "Acceptance or refusal of salvation...always occurs in an encounter with the world" (*TI*, V, 98).

3. *The difficulties of faith in modern culture.* Many factors converge to cause an eclipse of traditional and explicit faith, but a central cause lies in "the conditions surrounding human free action."[2] If faith is a decision, the pre–conditions and social supports for that decision have radically altered. Rahner often commented that in the older "homogeneous" or village-style society, the secular situation gave an artificial impression of widespread faith, and that in the new pluralist situations, which involve a dispersal (even a Babel) of centers of belonging, faith to survive has to become purified and more personal. In later years he stressed an honest agnosticism as "nothing other than the way in which God is experienced today" (*TI*, XXI, 133).

4. *The theological nature of atheism.* (a) It is all too easy today to deny God conceptually because of the hiddenness of God or the confusions of culture. In modern times it is a spiritual privilege to be able to hear the revelation of God fully and clearly, and hence unbelief today is "often merely objective"[3] sin: "Innocent atheism is always only categorial atheism, atheism on the plane of conceptual and propositional objectification" (*TI*, IX 158). (b) More serious is the situation of the nominal believer who in fact lives in unconverted egoism: "Theism can be the mask of a concealed atheism" (*TI*, IX 140). (c) A still deeper and morally culpable atheism stems from the refusal of God on the level of freedom—and thereby a choice to live in fundamental sin, closing mind and heart to love. Our whole existence is acceptance or rejection of the mystery we are. "God is always present to man in the dimension of transcendentality, and therefore can only be rejected by a free decision, not by knowledge as such" (*TI*, IX 158).

The crucial distinctions made by Rahner in an essay entitled "Atheism and Implicit Christianity" (in Volume 9 of *Theological Investigations*) can be simplified in the following table of four existential positions. There are two levels in each person, one existential or "transcendental" which is the key area for Rahner, the zone of fundamental options as lived. There is a second level, called the "categorial," which is greatly influenced by the surrounding culture and which involves a person's thought-out or voiced interpretations of life. In terms of faith in God, this second may often be in trouble in modern times but Rahner sees a "No" on the level of conceptual understanding as less theologically significant than the answer of either "Yes" or "No" on the deeper level of each person's existence.

Table of Four Stances		
	"Transcendental" i.e. implicit or lived	"Categorial" i.e. explicit or verbal
1. Fullness of Faith	YES	YES
2. Merely nominal belief	NO	YES
3. Culpable or total atheism	NO	NO
4. Possibility of anonymous Christian	YES	NO

Unbeliever as Anonymous Christian

No discussion of Rahner's understanding of unbelief can avoid some attention to the famous theory of the "anonymous Christian." In interviews in his later years Rahner often expressed surprise that such a fuss had been caused by a relatively obvious insight: if one lives according to the best light of one's con-science, one's life cannot really be closed to God, even if one describes oneself as an agnostic or atheist. Rahner linked this with traditional theology of baptism by desire, or with St. Augustine's saying that "many whom God has, the Church does not have; and many whom the Church has, God does not have."[4] In other words, there are those "who merely think that they are not Christians, but who are in the grace of God" (*TI*, IV, 366). As already seen, faced with modern culture, Rahner stresses the secondariness of the conceptual (what we "merely think") and the theological centrality of the existential (what we truly live). Equally, on the basis of Vatican II concerning the salvation of the unbeliever, Rahner argued that there must be a "theism that is anonymous, non-thematic" and "accepted in freedom" (*TI*, XI, 177).

This notion, however, caused much controversy. For instance, Hans Urs von Balthasar in 1966 attacked Rahner as diminishing missionary zeal, as weakening the believer's position in dialogue with non-believers, and as exaggerating the love of neighbor at the expense of love of God. No doubt by way of response to various critics, Rahner refined his theory considerably and especially so from the mid-1960s onward. Earlier he was inclined to apply it liberally to all non-believers, but as time went on he tended to emphasize more the element of a costly conversion of life, an option of generosity in spite of not believing in God. He also came to insist that this positive way of understanding the salvific potential of the non-believer does not diminish the church's evangelizing mission: indeed the church has a) "a function towards atheists even before they have explicitly found and recognized the Church" and b) the church "has no choice but to struggle against this atheism with all legitimate means" (*TI*, XXI, 146-147).

For present purposes, perhaps a helpful way of presenting the issue of the anonymous Christian briefly is as an argument that involves a series of eight steps. Rahner himself never outlined such an order and yet it emerges clearly from his writings, especially in his late book *Foundations of Christian Faith.*

Approached in this way, it will become clear that the proposal is not a strategy of apologetics or of spiritual imperialism; instead it is a gradual and complex response to a specifically theological question, to the old problem of the salvation of the unbeliever, approached now with the tools of transcendental theology. To demonstrate this, I list, with deliberate brevity, eight stages of a developing insight.

Step 1: God wills all to be saved (cf 1 Tim. 2:4); this has been described as "a primary axiom in Rahner's theology."

Step 2: But Paul also insists on coming to the truth of the mediator Jesus Christ. How can this be reconciled with the "all" of God's will?

Step 3: It must imply that some kind of non-explicit faith is salvific.

Step 4: This may take the form of "obedience to one's moral conscience" (*FCF*, 343) but this cannot be identified with merely "natural morality" (152).

These first four points add up to a possibility of salvation for unbelievers as acknowledged in Vatican II. The remaining steps are Rahner's particular interpretation of how this is theologically understandable.

Step 5: Every human existence belongs within the realm of God's self-giving (the so-called "supernatural existential"). A state of graced existence is both universal and supernatural, even if not always thematized or recognized (*FCF*, 127).

Step 6: But this offer and gift requires a response. There can be an implicit acceptance of transcendental revelation through the basic option guiding a person's whole life (*FCF*, 172).

Step 7: This act of responsibility cannot remain hidden. It involves a costly "Yes" to love and an implicit conversion to Christ (*FCF*, 296). To refuse this self-transcendence is also possible and would mean rejection of one's transcendental experience of God (*FCF*, 48).

Step 8: Thus one can speak of an anonymous search for Christ, even by the unbeliever, and one concretely embodied in love of neighbor, readiness for death, and hope for the future (*FCF*, 295-297).

From this progressive analysis, it should be obvious that this theory is far from cheap, that it envisages a demanding level of conversion, and that it suggests a second strand in the history of salvation for those who, for various reasons, cannot come to the privileged knowledge of God in Christ that is fullness of faith.

Pastoral Approach of "Mystagogy"

Whereas the phrase "anonymous Christian" became part of the jargon of theology in recent decades, the concept of "mystagogy" received much less attention. And yet this is Rahner's extension of his theory into the realm of pastoral practice with unbelievers. Even before he began to use the term, Rahner frequently insisted, as in 1954, that "every apostolate is an uncovering of that Christianity which God in his grace has already hidden in the hearts of those who think they are not Christians" (*TI*, III, 371). He stressed that people can already be Christian before Christianity is communicated explicitly to them, and hence that preaching has the purpose of bringing them to recognize their true selves and what is already alive within them. In one early essay he commented that such an approach was simply the method of St. Paul on the Areopagus. From 1966 onward Rahner began to use the word "mystagogy" to refer to ways of unveiling basic religious experiences even in the lives of unbelievers.

From the early centuries of the church, the word retains echoes of initiation into mystery, and Rahner adapts this to the situation of the modern atheist. In a sense, it takes the place of a more rationalist apologetics of the existence of God, and instead focuses on the depth experiences and options of generosity that a person may be living out but remain unaware of. Rahner speaks of this mystagogy as essential for fundamental theology today—a "theology which from the outset takes as its starting point man's experience of himself" (*TI*, XII, 213). Thus the challenge is to find a language that will discern the experiences of grace in the existence of the anonymous Christian.

"This must necessarily consist in personal initiation and in arousing an inner experience of faith. This is even the case when someone asserts that he is unaware of any experience of faith and has no interest in such a phenomenon" (*TI*, XVI, 10).

[Mystagogy] "would describe and focus the attention of each individual in his concrete existence on…the experience of *transcendence*" (*FCF*, 59, my italics).

In a lecture of 1980 Rahner returned to this question of mystagogy, contrasting it with ways of talking about God that are "unworthy of belief" because they are so distant from lived experience and so locked into a narrow theism (*TI*, XXI, 148); he even suggested that a papal encyclical be devoted to atheism, adopting a new tone, because "a shift of emphasis in our proclamation is absolutely indispensable" (*TI*, XXI, 150). This pastoral shift is crucially represented by what he calls mystagogy, and it involves a dialogue of discernment that might be able to name the "anonymous" by bringing into the open those personal experiences of self-giving and of encounter with the calls of life that, theologically, involve the interaction of grace and freedom. Underlying this emphasis is Rahner's increasing uneasiness over proposing Christian faith to a secularized world in primarily doctrinal language. He remained shy of such traditional or direct evangelization and, with atheists in mind, concentrated in theory and practice on the non-explicit dimensions of faith and of unbelief.

Additional German Perspectives: Johann B. Metz

While the Second Vatican Council was still in its closing stages, the German theologian Johannes B. Metz published an article entitled "Unbelief as a Theological Problem"—a short text that proved seminal.[5] Instead of situating the issue of unbelief in apologetics or as a phenomenon on the margins of theology, Metz insisted that this theme be tackled as a question interior to theology, and one confronting the believer's own faith and existence. Behind his new emphasis was the fact that an older "direct unbelief" or "life in opposition to God" had given way to a much more widespread characteristic of modern culture—"a positive possibility of existence *without God.*"[6] If the previous style of anti-religious unbelief had required direct apologetics, this more recent "a-religious" unbelief seemed to require rather an indirect apologetic that confronts unbelief within the "self-understanding of belief."[7] No longer could it be acceptable to deal with unbelief as something safely outside us but rather as *intra nos.*

Paradoxically the modern cultural situation highlights the theological reality that unbelief is not just a historical accident but rather a permanent danger to belief and that this belongs to the very nature of faith. For Metz faith is not a "thing-like" possession but rather a precarious and endangered gift of grace, ever changing because it is lived out in the drama of existence. An older Catholic theology gave priority of emphasis to faith as credal content and as assent of the intellect, and hence it tended to underplay any fragility or unbelief. But it was equally part of the traditional analysis of faith to insist that it involves both human freedom and an inevitable darkness in this life. When these two latter dimensions are given proper weight, a basic unbelief within the experience of faith comes to the fore.

However, this presence of unbelief in the believer should not be reduced to the psychological. It affects not only the experience of faith but rather faith itself. In this respect Metz refers to two other key aspects in the theology of faith: its differentness and lack of concreteness as understood within the tradition of negative theology, and a contrasting characteristic—faith as something to be lived in the ordinary, an intersubjective relationship, an engagement of the total person in an option of love. He voices certain hesitations over an excessively "personalist" approach to faith—one which stresses the relationship between the individual soul and God. Instead he argues that "what is most personal" occurs not in the private realm of "monadic subjectivity" but in the drama of "accepted or refused brotherly love."[8]

In this light, faith is, on the one hand, beyond all words and concepts. On the other hand, as a way of life it is always tempted by "concupiscence" and hence is always insecure and unsteady in its fidelity. This is an existential analysis, stressing the unbelief of the believer, as *simul fidelis et infidelis*, at once believing and unbelieving; but this does not imply an "unbelief of belief."[9] In summary Metz highlights that before "this question becomes an apologetical question about the unbelief in others, it is anteriorly and more originally a question of the believer about his own belief. The believer considers the risk involved in his own belief.... The believer, by his search for the belief of the unbeliever, questions his (own) unbelief."[10]

Problems with Traditional Theism

Exactly twenty-five years later another German theologian gave a lecture on atheism and theism, with some striking parallels and contrasts to this paper of Metz. Dorothee Sölle's "The End of Theism" starts from the remark that "our situation is character-ized by a pragmatic, unmilitant and painless atheism" and goes on to quarrel with the usual assumptions of the debate between theism and atheism.[11] In ways reminiscent of the argument of Michael J. Buckley (summarized in the next chapter on North American insights), she dismisses the assumptions of theism as "no longer thinkable"—in the sense of envisaging "a supreme Being at the top of the pyramid of being" as the origin of order and of existence. Such a picture of God as controller is incapable, she claims, of doing justice to contemporary experience.

But this irrelevance of an older theism is not the only barrier to faith now: "Christians today experience an irreconcilable contradiction between the normal atheism of their world on the one hand and the real experiences of God on the other.... In reality atheism and theism are equally remote from an existential faith which shapes the way in which one lives." Sölle prefers to interpret this situation positively: the death of the "theistic God" opens up opportunities "to speak of God in a concrete way, in a way related to praxis."[12]

As she puts it in another essay, the usual question "Do you believe in God?" tends to assume a superficial and merely theoretical framework, and thus to evoke an I-It relationship (to use Buber's terminology). God becomes a substance rather than an event, an explanation rather than a source of conversion of life, a supreme object rather than the God of revelation. Hence a question more in keeping with the reality of experience would be "Do you live out God?"[13] God in this way will be found as an I-Thou relationship and as a meaning-to-be-lived-by-us, not a distant formula of truth. In this light perhaps much atheism reacts against superficial answers to superficial questions about God.

Sölle echoes the negative judgment found in other theologians today against the God of the philosophers and against the "predominance of Aristotelian thought" in theology. What she calls a "super-transcendence" is an "unrelated transcendence" and hence "goes against religious experience." Instead theology needs to explore "transcendence in immanence."[14] Similarly unhelpful is the over-emphasis on God as power, something that she views as the root of "authoritarian religion."[15] This latter term comes from Erich Fromm whom Sölle quotes as characterizing this paradigm of religion as fatalist, pessimistic about human potentials and ultimately repressive. By contrast, a genuinely Christian religion stresses union with God through Jesus and the call to fullness of human responsibility through the exercise of creative freedom. (Once again it is worth noting the parallels with François Varone, as mentioned in the chapter here on French approaches.)

Sölle also links her analysis of theism and atheism with feminist theology, arguing that "the communicability of experience" is crucial for feminist thinking and that it is central for any genuine dialogue of faith horizons. Going further, she connects atheism with male domination: insofar as the temptation of the "white male" is to avoid weakness and "experiences of suffering" or of anxiety, the basis for faith is absent. But an "experience-related liberation theology" opposes the "unrelated God"—an image of God so easily discarded by this male and objectivist mentality with its pretence to be neutral and scientific.[16] Sölle's contrary position is summed up in these words:

> Today, the dispute over whether God can be thought of beyond us as resting in himself and unrelated, or whether God is the relationship itself and can be thought of only as relationship, seems to me to be one of the most important arguments between male-patriarchal and feminist theology. Is sovereignty the essential characteristic of God—or is it the capacity for relationship?... Only if we understand [our] being needed by God do we really learn to think in a liberating way."[17]

The Relevance of the Trinity

As a final example from Germany, it is significant that one of the classic books of contemporary theology, Walter Kasper's *The God of Jesus Christ* (first published in German in 1982), begins and ends with some extensive attention to atheism.[18] Indeed, more than a third of the whole book keeps atheism in focus as its dialogue partner in the search for a trinitarian theology adequate for today. Kasper is acutely aware of writing in a period where the real ravages of unbelief show themselves as a nihilist loss of direction and desire. An older militant and self-confident unbelief has given way to a mood of emptiness within the culture that is harder to confront or reach.[19]

Kasper discerns three basic types of modern atheism, two of them linked to different ways of understanding "autonomy" today: because of the "autonomy of nature and the secular spheres" there is less need of a "God-hypothesis" in science or culture, and therefore one has methodological atheism; secondly, there is the "autonomy of the subject" and such an emphasis on human dignity that God seems an unacceptable interference. The third form, often dramatically nourished through harsh experiences of life, is the unbelief that arises as a protest against evil in the world.[20] Having surveyed these at some length he sums up the "predicament of theology" as follows:

> Modern atheism has put theology in a difficult position. Of particular importance here is mass atheism, a phenomenon unparalleled in past history; it regards the practical, if not theoretical denial of God or at least indifference to belief in God as being by far the most plausible attitude to take. As a result, theology has been stripped of its power to speak to people and to communicate with them. There are now no generally accepted images, symbols, concepts and categories with which it can make itself understood. [This crisis] of contemporary theology arises from the loss of the *praeambula fidei*, that is, of the presuppositions which faith needs if it is to be possible as faith.[21]

As Rahner complained, those presuppositions had become too rationalist, and he would argue that the "mystagogic" preambles urgently needed for today's culture are more spiritual, more psychological and more symbolic. As Kasper puts it, "we lack the language and the adequately developed categories that would enable us to speak unambiguously about God," and therefore "the real issue today is no longer primarily this or that truth but the very ability to believe"—it is a question of loss of the "dimension of mystery," or, in other words, "a far-reaching loss of religious experience."[22] To open again a valid road of religious experience, beyond the narrowing of experience to the empirical, it is necessary to renew the "symbol dimension of reality" as an avenue toward an "option for meaning."[23]

Walter Kasper moves on from this initial analysis of the God-question in contemporary culture to a final proposal of the specifically Christian answer as *the* surprise for atheists—one that is practically always unknown or unappreciated by them: "The trinitarian confession is the Christian answer to the challenge of modern atheism."[24] He argues that the "proclamation of the triune God is of the greatest pastoral importance" because it is precisely a non-trinitarian "theism" which was the target of enlightenment atheism.[25] It is worth adding that in recent decades Kasper is not alone among theologians in being spurred by atheism into a renewed presentation of the Trinity as the core of faith.[26]

Notes

1. "Atheism," in *Sacramentum Mundi: An Encyclopedia of Theology*, ed. Karl Rahner (New York: Herder & Herder, 1968), I, 117.

To reduce the complexity of the notes, quotations from the two works of Rahner, referred to frequently in this chapter, will appear with abbreviations in parenthesis in the text as follows: *TI* = *Theological Investigations*, 23 volumes (New York: Crossroad, 1961–1992); *FCF* = *Foundations of Christian Faith* (New York: Seabury Press, 1978).

2. Karl Rahner, *Mission and Grace* (London: Sheed and Ward, 1963), I 11.

3. *Sacramentum Mundi*, ibid., p. 121.

4. *Mission and Grace*, I, 51.

5. Johann Baptist Metz, "Unbelief as a Theological Problem," *Concilium* (Vol. I, No. 6, 1965), pp. 32–42.

6. P. 32.

7. P. 33.

8. P. 38.

9. P. 37.

10. P. 39.

11. Dorothee Sölle, *Thinking About God: An Introduction to Theology* (Philadelphia: Trinity Press International, 1990). The chapters in question here are "The End of Theism," pp. 171–182, and "Who Is Our God?" pp. 183–195.

12. All references are to pp. 171–172.

13. P. 186.

14. P. 173.

15. P. 177.

16. Pp. 178–179.

17. Pp. 181–182.

18. Walter Kasper, *The God of Jesus Christ*, trans. M.J. O'Connell (London: SCM Press, 1984).

19. P. 11.

20. P. 19.

21. P. 46.

22. Pp. 64, 65, 81.

23. P. 114.

24. P. 314.

25. P. 215.

26. Thus, Nicholas Lash, at the conclusion of his book *Easter in Ordinary* (Notre Dame: University of Notre Dame Press, 1990) proposes that a genuine reappreciation of the Trinity is the perfect corrective to false images and tendencies in the understanding of God (pp. 265–266). In fact he links the absence of a living pedagogy of the Trinity with the strength of some versions of atheism: it is "an indication of the extent to which, under the dominant influence of modern theism (and of the anthropologies which produce both this theism and its denials), the doctrine of God's Trinity has, in fact, largely ceased to function as our Christian frame of reference" (p. 277). And he adds: "The way 'beyond' atheism does not lie through argument or self-assertion, but through that occurrence of community which makes possible the worship, 'in the Spirit,' of the unknown God" (p. 283). An important book that came too late to be included in any detail here is : Pierre Piret, *Les athéismes et la théologie trinitaire* (Bruxelles: Institut d'Etudes Théologiques, 1994).

4
North American Insights

Three excellent books on atheism were published in the course of 1985-1988 by North American theologians. Although each author seems to have been unaware of the others' work, in fact their different approaches converge, and hence all three books can fruitfully be discussed together here.

Costly Mistakes in History

Michael J. Buckley's *At the Origins of Modern Atheism* (New Haven: Yale, 1987) is a lengthy examination in the history of ideas, taking as its focus the seventeenth and eighteenth centuries, mainly in France. It is a specialist work, quite detailed in its historical analysis, but its central argument casts considerable light on the agenda of theology-and-atheism even for today. (Even though James Turner's book was published in 1985, it seems best to summarize it later because it deals with a period after that explored by Buckley.)

It tells the story of a failure of nerve in theology, whereby Christian defenders of faith began to limit themselves to a narrowly philosophical field of argument and to forget the role of revelation and of religious experiences. A basic mistake was made when "Catholic theologians" (from Lessius to

Malebranche) "abandoned the religious figure of Jesus as the principal evidence for the reality of God" (41).[1] They fell into the trap of accepting the terms of debate as set by their atheistic opponents, usually enthusiasts for a mechanistic explanation of the natural universe. Similarly nominally Christian thinkers, like Descartes, tended to narrow the field to the empirical, so that God became just an off-stage guarantor for the physical universe.

Buckley insists that to understand the roots of atheism in the last few centuries, we have to pay attention "to the theism of the theologians and the philosophers" and thus to view the "atheism of their adversaries" (16) as a reaction to the narrow forms of theism on offer, and indeed to the internal contradictions of that theism, that pretended to represent Christianity but in fact was an impoverished version of it. The target of his critique is the attempt to defend the divine without reference to Christ.

More bluntly, Buckley claims that "the Churches were the soil of atheism" (38-39). Historically the seventeenth century was an age when the "wars of religion and the wrangling of theologians had discredited religion" (47). Against a crisis background, theologians abandoned the core of theology in their desire to defend the existence of God, but it was a reaction born of panic. Thus Christology or any sense of the Spirit in religious experience was thought to be irrelevant and atheism was responded to "as if it were a philosophic issue rather than a religious one" (47). The net result was that "Christianity entered into the defense of the existence of the Christian God without appeal to anything Christian" (67).

As a result of this "surrender to natural philosophy of the foundations of religion" (283), not only was theology defending, perhaps without realizing it, a pale shadow of the Christian God, but also the various forms of atheism then in the ascendent found it easy to attack this reduction of religious belief. Buckley argues that a history of atheism has also to be a history of the theisms to which it responds. Its meaning lies not in itself but in the theism it seeks to deny or dismantle. In short "modern theism" of an untheological kind lies "at the root of modern atheism" (338), and atheism is best "treated as a transition from theism" (339). The tragedy lay in the fact that theologians allowed themselves to be hijacked onto alien ground.

Turning to the weak theisms being defended, Buckley finds a constant internal "contradiction between form and content" (343) in the defense of religious truth. The content aims to defend Christian basics but the form is limited to nature philosophy. Therefore "the warrant for the personal God was the impersonal world...[in] place of a religious tradition in which the personal God was known primarily by personal communication" (343). At the heart of this abdication to philosophy, and more importantly to the empiricist philosophy of the day, was the "self-alienation of religion" (341). Attempts at Christian apologetics lost sight of Christ and defended the explanation of the universe as if this was defending the God of revelation.

Lacking any appeal "to participative religious experience," relegating spirituality to a lesser role than the philosophic affirmation of the existence of God, the sad reality was that excellent theologians "bracketed religion in order to defend religion" and avoided "any appeal to the witness of a person" (345). It was a most costly mistake not only of strategy but of Christian thinking. "Christianity, in order to defend its God, transmuted itself into theism" (346). Surrendering in this way, religion failed to trust its own authentic "cognitive claims" that need not restrict themselves to discourse about God "from the outside" (346), whereas "if religion has no intrinsic justification, it cannot be justified from outside" (360). That last sentence is not only a comment on a false turning in theological history, but an invitation to a new theology of faith that reverences the full human adventure of trying to believe and live in the light of Christ. Christianity faced with unbelief needs intellectual confidence in its own tools and in a form of specifically religious understanding that stays faithful both to the nature of faith and to the revelation of Christ.

In Buckley's words, "the Christian God cannot have a more fundamental witness than Jesus Christ.... Christian theology cannot abstract from Christology in order to shift the challenge for this foundational warrant onto philosophy" (361). But this has often happened—not only in the seventeenth century—with the result that faith has suffered a series of self-alienations from its own unique reality as rooted primarily in the person of Christ and grounded in "religious experience or personal witness, history, or event" (362).

In a separate treatment of the same area, Buckley explores again how a merely deductive or externalist approach to the question of God's existence can in fact foster atheism, and he voices the positive side of his argument more strongly than in his book:

> In turning to some other discipline to give basic substance to its claims that God exists, religion...is admitting an inner cognitive emptiness. If religion does not possess the principles and experiences within itself to disclose the existence of God, if there is nothing of cogency in the phenomenology of religious experience, the witness of the personal histories of holiness and religious commitment, the sense of claim by the absolute already present in the givenness of God, an awareness of the infinite horizon opening up before inquiry and longing, an awakening jolted into a more perceptive consciousness by limit-experiences, the long history of religious institutions and practice, or the life and meaning of Jesus of Nazareth, then it is ultimately counterproductive to look outside of the religious to another discipline or science or art to establish that there is a "friend behind the phenomena." Inference cannot substitute for experience, and the most compelling witness to a personal God must itself be personal. To attempt something else either as foundation or as substitute...is to move into a process of internal contradiction of which the ultimate resolution is atheism.[2]

Thus Buckley's historical investigation is of considerable pastoral relevance: it says, in effect, that one dominant form of philosophical atheism caused a side-tracking of faith and of theology into a dangerously rationalist mold, and that ironically this narrowing of the theological agenda only increased the likelihood of more atheism. "Only connect" was the motto chosen by E. M. Forster for his novel *Howards End*; the shrunken God that emerged from these intellectual debates could never connect with the spiritual experiences at the heart of Christianity or with the passionate hungers at the core of people's lives. Religion betrayed itself in a loss of nerve. God became incredible because God became small. It is not an unusual happening today.

McLelland and the Promethean Impulse

Joseph McLelland's *Prometheus Rebound: The Irony of Atheism* (Waterloo: Wilfrid Laurier University Press, 1988) also sees modern atheism as "committed to the theology of classical theism in its counter arguments" (62) and holds that in this respect "antitheism assumes something about the Christian God that is not so" (286). Thus Buckley and McLelland agree that much atheism is born from a mistaken image of God, and that Christian thinkers and preachers were often responsible for those false images. Both writers would echo a statement of Alisdair MacIntyre that "the God in which the nineteenth and early twentieth centuries came to disbelieve had been invented only in the seventeenth century" (cited by McLelland, 11). Even more striking is the fact that both point in much the same direction for religious solutions to the dilemma of atheism. We have just quoted Buckley stressing the role of "participative" experiences as an antidote to a deistic notion of belief or unbelief; McLelland also suggests that theism needs "revision" in the direction of "participation" and a "renewed concept of covenant" (286). Where false images of God abound, and especially when these imply a God without love, the obvious pastoral remedy lies in the recognition of a God of incarnation and companionship.

As McLelland puts it, there was a "foundational category mistake" in antitheism, where "the divine is by definition a Tyrant

(292, 15), and his version of a shrunken God is more psychological than philosophical. Where Buckley bemoans the cramping of God into the narrow terms of the nature philosophy dominant during the seventeenth century and later, McLelland draws on the long and fascinating history of the Prometheus myth as a summarizing image of atheistic rebellion. Where Buckley examines a conflict of ideas in two crucial centuries, McLelland opts for a broader drama of images through many ages and stages of western culture.

There are many versions of the myth of the rebellion of Prometheus against Zeus and of his stealing of the fire on behalf of humanity. Differences aside, the key issue is one of defiance against a dictator God. When the revolt of Prometheus is punished is various ways (tied to a rock and having his liver eaten by an eagle), it only magnifies the sense of anger against the injustice of a divinity of such jealousy and willfulness. Thus Prometheus becomes a central symbol in western culture of the humanist rejection of an inhuman, distant, and oppressive God. If God is like Zeus, will not everyone want to imitate Prometheus? Yes, answers McLelland, adding that all too often even the Christian God was imaged as more akin to Zeus of "arbitrary dictates" (40) than the real God of revelation.

Whether or not they make explicit mention of Prometheus, something of this stance of rebellion lies behind many of the classical philosophers of atheism. Thus Karl Marx spoke of Prometheus as "the noblest of saints and martyrs in the calendar of philosophy" (25) and Bertrand Russell dismissed the idea of God as a "conception derived from the ancient Oriental despotisms... quite unworthy of free men" (5). But it should be added that a whole tradition of Christian commentators—from Tertullian to William Lynch—interpreted Prometheus as a Christ figure suffering for humanity and inviting people into creative freedom. On the other hand Thomas Merton used the symbol of Prometheus negatively—as a religion of Pelagian and willful selfhood that has to snatch the gift "when God is not looking" (42).

The problem lies not so much in Prometheus as in the Zeus that he has to defy. If this "retired Architect" or "distant Enemy" (279, 291) is present in the images of God, a conflict of wills results and some version of atheism becomes not only inevitable but justified. At the heart of this mythic struggle is the question of human autonomy and of divine providence, and the Christian answer is found only through Christ. In his closing pages McLelland confronts this history of Promethean atheism with Christian theology, and again, in parallel fashion to Buckley, notes the need for an adequate Christology as a response. Too often a "Monophysite doctrine of Christ as divine intruder" (280) has passed itself off as orthodoxy, with the result that the human struggles within Jesus were downplayed. Another source of trouble lies in the notion of divine omnipotence, often reduced to "all-mightiness, power to do anything" (281). Against the Zeus-like capricious or despotic God, the Canadian theologian prefers an expression of John Macquarrie about the "overwhelmingness of God" (285).

Finally, for McLelland, it is Karl Barth that provides the best antidote to the false drama of Zeus and Prometheus. He cites some of the eloquent passages where Barth argues that rational thought in theology need not and should not exclude such qualities as gratitude, reverence and love: without a necessary receptivity of response we are in danger always of a "nostrification" of God, whereby we become, so to speak, the managers of revelation rather than its disciples. "This is why the atheistic negative— which negates only a God who, if he exists, has to be a 'datum' of ours—does not touch him" (cited 290). And Barth adds, in a spirit of self-confession, that there is an ever-present form of atheism within the believer—"the fact that we are not better Christians": the "atheism that is the real enemy is the 'Christianity' that professes faith in God very much as a matter of course, perhaps with great emphasis, and perhaps with righteous indignation at atheism wild or mild, while in its practical thinking and behaviour it carries on exactly as if there were no God" (cited 289).

A Specifically American Perspective

James Turner's *Without God, Without Creed: The Origins of Unbelief in America* (Baltimore: Johns Hopkins University Press, 1985) tackles the American history of unbelief but arrives at conclusions that closely parallel those of Buckley. Although the authors he cites are quite different, the pattern in the carpet is much the same. Why did belief in God become a subculture of the majority of Americans? There is no contradiction in that last sentence: most Americans *privately* believe in God, but the public and shared culture of the United States is not unified or much influenced by that faith; indeed it seems more controlled by secular and agnostic assumptions. Thus what is personally important to many has become a subculture. Or, in Everett Ladd's striking phrase, "America is today what it has always been: a highly religious, intensely secular society."[3]

Like Buckley, Turner argues that also in America the "parents of modern unbelief turn out to have been the guardians of belief" (261), and their fatal mistake in Turner's analysis lay also in a rationalized argument that "forgot the transcendence essential to any worthwhile God" (267). Thus what religion became under the pressures of American modernity actually caused unbelief. Gradually the American defenders of faith— through the eighteenth and nineteenth centuries—downplayed both revelation and the role of mystery in religion, and ended up with a worldly religion, and with a humanized and split God. On the one hand there was an over-confidence in science as the "high road to certainty" concerning God (58), and this developed into a "lust for empirical proof" that eventually was "nothing less than disastrous for belief" (189). On the other hand "belief" became cut off from "faith," with the first term suggesting a narrowly cognitive approach to God-as-verifiable-proposition and the second becoming watered down into a vague trust in moral goodness. The argument that "belief in God was entirely reasonable and plausible" (29) held sway in different forms until the mid-nineteenth century, and then whereas "in 1850, the intellectual ground of belief in God had seemed like bedrock, by 1870 it felt more like gelatin" (199). In those years, a host of new questions—about evolution and about the Bible in particular— found the older defenses unable to cope, and largely because of the "rationalized and moralized belief" espoused by different generations of its defenders had unconsciously robbed Christian faith of its core of revelation.

In Turner's judgment, the ways of defending faith against the new problems that surfaced from 1500 to 1900 were paradoxically responsible for the agnosticisms that emerged as the most "moral" option for a whole generation of intellectual Americans in the late nineteenth century. The nature of knowledge had changed and the theologians were caught unprepared. In Turner's own words,

> This new epistemological model had deep historic roots: in the process of secularization that had pried apart natural and supernatural, in the economic changes that had created a new social basis for understanding reality, in the shaping of a powerful new science, and in the strategies of religious leaders who wanted above all else to make God find man's new world.... Already rendered intellectually incredible and morally repugnant, belief in God thus faded in favor of an entirely human morality and a religion of this world (pp. 195, 259).

Notes

1. In order to reduce the notes, in this chapter where the page references are clearly to particular books, they will be given in parenthesis in the text.

2. Michael J. Buckley, "Newtonian Settlement and Atheism," in *Physics, Philosophy and Theology*, ed. R.J. Russell, W.R. Stoeger, and G.V. Coyne (Vatican City: Vatican Observatory, 1988), pp. 81–102. Quotation on p. 99.

3. *Unsecular America*, ed. Richard J. Neuhaus (Grand Rapids: Eerdmans, 1986), p. 23.

5
Contrasting Perspectives: Montreal and Paris

Language of Local Cultures

As mentioned in the introduction, a Secretariat for Non-Believers was founded in the Vatican in 1965, and a quick summary of its concerns was given. This Roman office encouraged the setting up of local centers to reflect on more specific issues of unbelief in different situations. Two of these are of particular interest, a center founded in Paris in 1966 and another in Montreal in 1970. Both have remained active through the years, and each publishes a regular periodical on issues of unbelief.[1]

The differences in theological and pastoral emphasis can be stated in summary form: Paris put much emphasis on network groups of mutual exchange between believers and unbelievers, and in these encounters the topics that often arose were: the search for meaning as an lived experience; listening and auto-critique by the church; dialogue of action and values rather than of ideas; the radical changes in culture that followed on 1968. A typical statement of approach can be cited from Bishop Jean Honoré, President of the Paris center, from 1979: "Our quest is to define the conditions of an affirmation of God in the culture which we share with unbelievers."[2]

By contrast, Montreal found itself faced with a quite different challenge—the rapid secularization of a previously highly Catholic culture in French-speaking Canada, and hence a key concern became "distanciation" from the church and how to understand it. The Montreal center set itself goals of research into the process of how unbelief develops, of dialogue with unbelievers, and of animation of training sessions of various kinds for the "sensibilization" of believers.

Unbelief and Theology

Because André Charron, the theologian principally linked with the Montreal "Service Incroyance et Foi," did a major piece of historical research on France itself, his work can serve as both introduction and bridge between the two situations. Charron's extensive historical study of modern theology vis-à-vis atheism, *Les Catholiques face à l'athéisme contemporain*, was published in 1973 and examines in detail the evolution of thought concerning unbelief by French theologians between 1945 and 1965. However, for the purposes of this survey, we will limit ourselves to Charron's fifth chapter where he moves beyond the historical to speculate toward a yet-to-be-elaborated "theology of atheism". He proposes various perspectives as fundamental for such a project.

(1) Any such theology of atheism should be an essential part of fundamental theology today and, paradoxically, it should be part of a theology of the act of faith and its essential freedom.[3]

(2) This theological reflection on unbelief needs to focus on faith and unbelief in terms of a developing process of life stances, a decision rooted in various dispositions.[4]

(3) Adopting an anthropological method, it would need to examine the human experience of questioning, of doubting and of personal appropriation of meaning.[5]

(4) In this respect, Charron offers a full discussion of the causes of unbelief under four sub-headings: (a) permanent sources of atheism such as the non-obviousness of God or the

existence of evil; (b) contemporary pressures such as the crisis of truth, or the ambivalent spin-off from a technological culture; (c) historical reasons such as the desacralizing of the modern society or the failures of believers to have the courage of their faith. (d) psychological reasons within the personal story of each individual or the forgetting of God as a superfluous distraction.[6] Later he adds that a theology of unbelief must include "an ecclesiological chapter" because the human face of the church can be a counter-witness and source of unbelief.[7]

(5) There is room for a philosophical and rational defense of the existence of God, but the traditional proofs need to be reworked in more existential language and to examine in personalist ways the conditions for inner assent to the reality of faith.[8]

(6) Highlighted by the pressures of unbelief, the core of the act of faith is seen all the more clearly as both recognition and option.[9]

Throughout the years Charron has published many articles on aspects of unbelief and of pastoral responses to it in which he applies these pointers of his book. Frequently he adopts a developmental model of analysis, in order to clarify different levels of crisis of faith. Thus it is important not to confuse non-practice with unbelief, and yet how are they connected? Its abandonment can be significant but one needs to realize that it is only one of several dimensions of an ideally integrated faith: "The abandonment of liturgical practice can lead to the numbing of Christian practice, that is to say, of a faith alive in deeds... through distance from any community of support, from any pedagogy in the meeting with God, with his word, and with the sacraments."[10] Nevertheless to isolate the dimension of church-going is to run the risk of ritualism. Other dimensions of faith include the moral, the doctrinal, the social and the spiritual.[11]

Challenge of Apathy

If we turn to his important and more recent article concerning religious indifference in Canada, Charron proposes some distinctions between key terms, unbelief being "the absence or rejection of religious faith, as option and as system of beliefs," non-belief implying more absence than denial, and indifference being "the absence not only of beliefs and of religious faith but also of all questioning in matters of religion." As such he sees it as the "most radical form of unbelief." In the French Canadian situation it can be present among "cultural Christians" who still come to church for various rites of passage.[12]

Charron examines the causes of such unbelief without content, and he lists the "pluralism of options" fostered by modernity allied to the cultural uprooting characteristic of contemporary urban settings with their breakdown of natural communities. If, in classical modernity, religion was relegated to the margins of society, in post-modernity one lives with an even greater primacy of the solitary ego together with all the pressures of a "supermarket" of values beyond the influence of religious institutions. Collectively, therefore, recent years have witnessed a transition from a "society of prescription" to a "society of inscription"—in the sense that one must make a choice if one is to avoid drifting, but drifting seems the more typical fate of many.[13]

What might be some pastoral guidelines in the face of such deep indifference? Charron offers four main pointers in this respect.

(1) He insists on a human preparation of the ground, on the need to help a person get in touch with the basic values of his or her existence, before being able to arrive at any option of faith. Indifference, almost by definition, is closed to questing and hence a whole process of awaking of possibilities must be given priority.[14]

(2) Charron adds that since many people have vague and distorted notions of religion in their memories, it is often crucial to "undertake a critique of religion" in order to get rid of misunderstandings and blockages.[15]

(3) In such situations of unbelief, Christian beliefs will be communicated best through the "anthropological categories of

culture today" and in particular by seeing Jesus Christ as "a personal God recognized within the horizon of gratuitous love," someone who invites people to join his "project of the kingdom of God."[16]

(4) If the victim of indifference is to find his or her way toward lived faith, it will need a strong pastoral emphasis on "companionship in spiritual searching" and the church as "offering places of recomposition"—where support and gradual rebuilding of a vision can take place.[17]

Psychological Training for Dialogue

At the Montreal Service Incroyance et Foi, the theological reflection of André Charron has been paralleled by the work of Léopold de Reyes, who took a more psychological angle on the phenomenon of unbelief and by the mid 1980s had gathered data from over two thousand workshops of his own creation, called "Approche Dialogale" (dialogic approach). His reflections were published over the years mainly in the journal of the Service Incroyance et Foi, *Nouveau Dialogue.*

De Reyes starts from the thesis that every person has a "theologal relational potential" which is the basis of any experience of the living God. Just as everyone has a social potential for language, a cosmic potential for contact with the world, and a psychic potential for awareness, so each one has a theologal potential for conversion to God. This anthropology links up with studies of the sense of the sacred or of humanity as "capax Dei," as radically open to God.[18] But in the light of modern humanist psychology, de Reyes puts most emphasis on the unconscious *attitudes* that can often underlie explicit religious commitments or their absence. What it is that can block the development of this orientation toward integration and mature conversion? In this light he approaches especially the phenomenon of practical unbelief or religious indifference.

A key answer that emerges is in terms of "repression" of

"anxiety" in the religious dimension of the unbeliever. The very question of God naturally rouses anxiety but many "unconsciously convert this anxiety into attitudes that are defensive, aggressive, superstitious or simply through repression." In this way they create an insensibility to the question of faith, and fall into what is usually called practical atheism or religious indifference.[19] Behind these reactions can be a whole series of causes: images of a terrifying or devouring God; the unconscious decision to efface the question of God or else to struggle against a hostile God; defense mechanisms against existential anxiety that express themselves as philosophical agnosticism.[20] De Reyes concludes that what appears as tranquil unbelief on the surface often masks a psychological forgetting of the question, and hence that this practical atheism "is not of the philosophic or cognitive type" but rather is "affective" and "axiological," rooted in an avoidance of anxiety over either believing or not believing. Often, he adds, only some "emotive shock" or crisis of suffering will awaken people to be able to face their ignored existential anxieties and to bridge the distance they have created between themselves and possible faith in God.[21]

The French Analysis

Jean-François Six was the leading thinker of the Paris Secretariat for Non-Believers in its early years. Against the particular background of the French emphasis on a major crisis of culture, the title of his book *L'Incroyance et la foi ne sont pas ce qu'on croit* is itself indicative of his thesis that fresh interpretations and responses were needed. As early as 1979, he discerned the death of "old-fashioned atheism with its own certitudes" and the birth of a new "paganism."[22] In Six's view the basis of unbelief changed drastically after about 1960. Up to then, it was commonly linked to an older version of scientism, with a dominance of positivist seeing. But the new culture had rebelled against such rationalization and now the new obstacle to believing came rather from an "ocean of uncertainties that make people suspicious of choices" on offer and moving rather toward a new "recourse to the irrational."[23] A new generation finds itself less at home in the old humanism and more inclined to values of a creative and affective kind, which can even develop into a "gnostic mentality."[24] (These comments were made long before New Age was heard of, at least in France, and thus Six was prophetic of a face of unbelief that was yet to emerge.)

In a second chapter, Six moves from this cultural analysis to reflect on more theological aspects. Starting from the experience of mystical darkness by Saint Thérèse of Lisieux, who spoke of eating at the table of unbelievers, invaded by "an impenetrable darkness,"[25] he goes on to identify how faith must now live "the presence of God as an absence,"[26] and how throughout the gospels Jesus was attacked by a *religious* form of unbelief, the continuing history of which "is yet to be written."[27] The gospel of John in particular offers a long reflection on the reality that "belief is not natural" to humanity, and that "belief and unbelief are not in a formula, but in the heart."[28] In the light of Six's reading of John, unbelief is more normal, and faith involves a perpetual struggle for authenticity in the teeth of many traps of religious self-deception.

Thus, in his remaining chapters, Six examines the situation of "post-atheism" as a challenge to rediscover the always more difficult path of genuine Christian faith. The primary form of unbelief is not the post-enlightenment denial of God by the mind, but rather the tendency, even among so-called believers, to possess God and even to remain ignorant of the depth of their unbelief. Indeed Six sees the deeper history of unbelief as involving the history of the church itself: "The God who has all too often been presented by the Churches, as a matter of fact, has been a simple product of deists. He is a being who organizes the universe and the existence of humankind through a certain number of imperatives."[29]

Against such a God of destiny, often approached with a false rationality, Jesus is always "subversive," inviting people to believe in a vulnerable and unexpected God, who is "Tenderness and Happiness."[30] The real God of mystery is encountered as relationship rather than omnipotent "guarantor of order."[31] This God of "gratuitousness" can easily seem superfluous because of a natural and superficial desire for a more useful deity. That we "want constantly to escape the night" is the root of the deeper and more perennial unbelief.[32] Under the pressure of the new culture, these false securities fostered by some kinds of religious belief become sources of unbelief. The answer, for Six, lies not in defending a "pragmatic-sufficient truth" but in acknowledging the fragility of faith, and in speaking "of God with extreme modesty" because God "is wholly a poem and not a demonstration."[33]

Reacting to a Religion of Fear

There are many likenesses between Six's approach and that found in a 1981 book by François Varone: *Ce Dieu Absent qui fait Problème—Religion, athéisme et foi: trois regards sur le Mystère.*[34] This book, which has now gone through several editions, represents a pastoral approach to the absence of God in contemporary life. Rather like Six, Varone is a severe critic of the survival of an old law-based religion even within Christianity. In somewhat similar fashion to Buckley and McLelland, he sees atheism as born from a reduction of Christian revelation—in this case to a religion of fear. Indeed he uses the term "religion" in an exclusively negative sense, where it might have been better to choose a phrase such as "impoverished religion." In his view this distortion of Christian reality starts from an emphasis on human weakness, and seeks to bargain with God's power; thus religion tends to become merely a form of security to protect us against a potentially hostile God.

Where this agenda of faith dominates people's images of God, they lose touch with revelation as gift, with love and covenant, and with God's hopes to liberate our humanity for the kingdom. Where religion plugs into fear, it is incapable of dealing adequately with the paradoxical hiddenness and closeness of God as at once absent and present. In Varone's analysis different distortions of religion give rise to different kinds of atheism. Thus a "religion of fear," basing itself on law and cultivating guilt, clashes sooner or later with the sense of human autonomy, and hence an "existentialist atheism" is born. In a different way a "religion of utility," basing itself on ritualism, clashes with the evolving scientific sense of the world, and a "practical atheism" is born. "Christianity falls back quickly into religion."[35]

Such inadequacies leave themselves open to being dismissed by atheists as projections. In fact they *are* projections. Here God is imaged as sometimes (and rather capriciously) interfering to answer human desire and to change events. This God is a quasi-magical power, controlling, demanding, and even potentially sadistic. On the other hand the key to "faith" is that it starts from the surprise of God's revelation. The initiative is God's and the call is to freedom, love, creativity, partnership, responsibility for history. The only genuine "interference" of God takes the form of the person of Jesus. In this light, "faith" (as opposed to "religion") is able to cope with the felt absence of God, because it recognizes the mystery of God's silence as a factor of reverence for human freedom. Faith is rooted in trust but not in total security: "Alienation of freedom is often tranquillizing but freedom itself is not."[36]

For Varone a conversion from religion to faith is crucial today if a person is to arrive at a mature and livable Christianity. It means leaving behind the "false God pleased-by-duty and by fear, the facile and useful God of efficacious rites" in order to discover the true God "who exists so that I may exist, who gives an overall meaning to my life so that I can fill out that meaning for myself and for others, the One who gives meaning to my responsibility, searching, doubts and plans. One has to begin to exist in order to be a believer." "One becomes and remains a believer insofar as one knows oneself loved by God."[37] In brief, Varone views atheism as intimately connected with impoverishments in religion and hence responds to it with a purified journey into genuine faith.

A Deeper Credibility Gap

As a final and sober example from France, there is a recent article by the French Dominican, Jean-Pierre Jossua, where he argues that a massive indifference reigns in Europe concerning religion.[38] He views it as so deep a crisis that those older pastoral responses that stressed "witness" and a sharing of existence now appear weak. He goes on to doubt the optimistic assumption that the desire for God is universal and only awaiting to be awakened. And in his view, contemporary unbelief cannot be adequately understood as a product of materialism and individualism: some of the most generous, creative and spiritual people of today have no time for religion or for faith. Besides, there is a whole new "floating religiousness" that offers people enticing spiritual experiments without any stable belonging or commitment; this new emotional "credulity" is hostile to any definite revelation.[39]

The depth of the crisis of faith in contemporary culture, according to Jossua, is radically different from even some decades ago. If the advance warning signs began in the 1950s, we are now faced with generations who lack any social contact with religion, and whose imagination remains empty of living religious memories or symbols. Jossua locates the crisis therefore in a kidnap of the imagination by shallow and consumerist attitudes and in a resultant gulf of credibility between people and the Christian tradition of belonging and of revelation. In this moment that he describes as "nocturnal," he sees some fragile signs of hope: new forms of community and of belonging; openings to transcendence at key moments of life; ways of invitation to the gospel vision that do not seem unduly "total" or tightly controlling; expressions of Christian meaning, praxis and spirituality that do not fall into the merely glib or emotional.[40]

Notes

1. The "Service Incroyance et Foi" of Montreal publishes *Nouveau Dialogue* five times a year, and the Service Incroyance-Foi of Paris publishes *Incroyance et Foi* four times a year.

2. *Incroyance et Foi*, No. 11, 1979, p.3.

3. André Charron, *Les Catholiques face à l'athéisme contemporain* (Montreal: Fides, 1973), p.526.

4. P. 570.

5. P. 580.

6. Pp. 516-523.

7. Pp. 580-581.

8. Pp. 556-557.

9. Pp. 560.

10. *Une Pratique Dominicale et Chrétienne à Redécouvrir* (Montreal: Fides, 1975), p. 19.

11. A' propos de la foi ou de l'incroyance des jeunes: une grille de lecture, *Nouveau Dialogue* (No 12, Août 1975) p. 27.

12. André Charron, "Situation dé l'incroyance et de l'indifférence religieuse au Canada: analyse et perspectives pastorales," *Atheism and Faith* (Pontifical Council for Dialogue with Non-Believers: Vatican), XXVI, 4, 1991, pp. 264-265.

13. Pp. 267-268

14. P. 270.

15. P. 270.

16. P. 271.

17. P. 273.

18. Leopold de Reyes, "La foi et le potentiel relationnel théologal de l'être humain: étude sur la psychologie de l'expérience religieuse," in *Questions Actuelles sur la Foi*, ed. T. Potvin (Montreal: Fides, 1984), pp. 123-150.

19. de Reyes, "Une interprétation psychologique de l'athéisme pratique," *Nouveau Dialogue* (No. 54, mars 1984), pp. 24-28. Quotation translated from p. 26.

20. P. 27.

21. P. 28.

22. This book was translated into English: *Is God Endangered by Believers*, trans. T. Attanasio (Denville: Dimension Books, 1983), p. 6.

23. Pp. 31-32.

24. P. 42.

25. P. 47.

26. P. 50.

27. P. 57.

28. Pp. 60, 64.

29. P. 70.

30. P. 86.

31. P. 117.

32. P. 126.

33. P. 137.

34. *Ce Dieu absent qui fait problème* (Paris: Cerf, 1981).

35. Pp. 51, 41.

36. P. 69.

37. Pp. 62, 66.

38. Jean-Pierre Jossua, "La théologie devant l'incroyance," *Incroyance et Foi* (Quarterly of the Service Incroyance-Foi, No. 63-64, 1992), pp. 29-35.

39. P. 32.

40. Pp. 33-34.

6
Hispanic Approaches

Spanish-language thinking on unbelief, whether emerging from Spain or Latin America, has some characteristics that are not so strongly present in other cultures. There is emphasis on unbelief in its sociological dimension, and this against a recent history where the church was more strongly influential in public life. Connected with this there is also much attention given to the transition from "modernity" to "post-modernity." Both these issues are explored in other parts of the world, but they seem to be more constant and central issues in Spanish-language theological reflection in recent years. Together with this debate on pluralism and on post-modernity, there is the different approach of liberation theologians to the topic of unbelief. This chapter will begin with this latter stance.

Liberation Approaches

Liberation theology often distinguishes between two implied audiences. European theology, even in its more "progressive" mold, wants to address the "non-believers" of western culture, but a liberation theology is committed to the "non-persons," to the majority in the third world who are victims of injustice. Because the socio-cultural contexts are so different, the assumptions, the methods, and the targets of the two theologies remain radically different.

From a liberation standpoint, concern with unbelief can be seen as a question of individual meaning, but concern with injustice involves praxis in the light of revelation. Western-style theologizing on unbelief is sometimes judged to be too preoccupied with a privatized and secularized consciousness, whereas liberation theology tries to critique those aspects of modernity that both exploit the poor and shield the rich from the challenge of the gospel. Thus one needs to expose the idolatry in the "tacit atheism of consumerist society."[1] Another expression of this stance would argue that the main question "is not so much whether God exists, but which is the true God." In this light the God problem "is not so much atheism but idolatry," and certain images of God can tranquillize the comfortable believer against the radicality of Christian conversion.[2]

Gustavo Gutiérrez, as one of the leaders in the field, illustrates this insistence that the unbelief agenda of European theology is not a key issue for liberation theology. His approach is to start from concrete commitment within the struggles of the poor and from that stance to evolve a worthy language for speaking about God. "In Latin America things are different": that one sentence is the basis of his self-distancing from the typical concerns of the secularized world.[3]

> Liberation theology's first question cannot be the same one that progressivist theology has asked since Bonhoeffer. The question is not how we are to talk about God in a world come of age, but how we are to tell people who are scarcely human that God is love.... Liberation theology categorizes people not as believers or unbelievers but as oppressors or oppressed.... The interlocutors of progressivist theology question faith; the interlocutors of liberation theology "share" the same faith as their oppressors, but do not share the same economic, social, or political life. But in [the] light of God's word, faith cannot be separated from historical reality.[4]

In short, where "unbelief theology" assumes a situation where faith is under threat amid the complexities of new styles of culture, society, and ways of thought, "liberation theology" opts to give attention to a less internalized danger and destruction— the "underside of history," the "wretched of the earth." By comparison with such daily tragedies of human beings, the challenge of unbelief is judged to be a crisis within a comfortable society, and therefore of less interest and urgency within the horizon of the third world.

Even such a brief summary forces one to see this whole field in a different light. Yes, unbelief *is* largely a concern of the richer world. Indeed the decline of religious faith in the first world could be said to be a by-product of its own complex history—a history that is not only religious but intellectual, cultural, social, political and economic. The explosion of affluent life-styles within recent generations has seemed to rob people of the spiritual freedom necessary for faith. The typically lost or lonely searcher of the "developed" world, as so often presented in literature or movies, inhabits a different universe to the poor peasants of the third world. For these latter, community is often strong and God seems very real. Hence, understandably, many liberation theologians keep a certain distance from the theme of unbelief, suspecting it of being a problem mainly for the so-called developed world.

Unbelief as Culturally Conditioned

Turning back to more "western" concerns, in 1988 in Spain two works appeared that approach unbelief through reflection on its cultural roots: *Increencia y evangelización* by Juan Martín Velasco and *Raíces Culturales de la increencia*, a booklet of some forty-five pages by José Gómes Caffarena.

Caffarena's work deals with three families of influences in contemporary culture: the empiricist mentality, the humanist sensibility, and the link between pragmatism and indifference. In the historical background of empiricism lies a long story of post-enlightenment thinking that coincided with the success story of the scientific revolution. Thus was born a positivist tendency that dismissed religion as myth and something humanity would soon outgrow. And this sense of humanity come of age remains influential even in this late twentieth century and is bolstered by the idea that unless there is tangible evidence for God, religious faith is beyond logic and lacks intellectual seriousness. In Caffarena's words, "The dispute of the philosophers here echoes very directly what many people live inside themselves. What believer has never had at least the desire to see a miracle that would confirm faith?"[5] The pressures of an empiricist culture force believers to acknowledge that God is a non-scientific hypothesis, and that there can be other intelligent foundations for faith beyond the narrowly empirical realm. But there is no doubt that the subtle pressures of an empirical mode of thinking leaves many believers shaky in their faith.

The humanist model of unbelief also has a strong history in the nineteenth century, ranging from the Feuerbach-style rejection of God in the name of human greatness to the Marxist dismissal of God as an escape from historical responsibility. Caffarena sees this whole tradition of atheism as "Promethean" or as expressing a "Sisyphus" model of frustration. But he proposes that the most widespread humanism in contemporary culture is better described as the Dionysus model: in its "post-modern" form it abandons the search for a single unifying meaning for life and seems content with partial experiences. It exalts spontaneity, rejects morality and fixed truth, and, disenchanted with the "modernist" hopes of technological solutions for human problems, offers young people a cult of anchorless freedom that can even include spirituality. Thus it becomes a kind of anti-humanism, advocating the so-called "death of man," in the sense of letting go of the enlightenment project of the individual subject. In Caffarena's judgment this cynical post-modernism is one of the most severe challenges to religious faith today, since to abandon the value of the human being is to deny one of the essential characteristics of the Christian vision.[6]

Turning to his third aspect of unbelief, Caffarena argues that the indifference that is found in modern culture does not affect only the religious dimension. It stems from a sense of failure and impotence before the many ideals of history—toward progress, security, well-being, justice, economic management. Above all this, indifference is connected with "a crisis of ideologies"[7] and especially the collapse of collectivist dreams. A second root of indifference can be discerned in the dominance of "immediacy" and privatized living in welfare societies. "Neither God nor any ultimate has much possibility today to capture our interest beyond the barrier of attractions that are much nearer."[8] In competitive and neocapitalist cultures, the very capacity for inner searching can shrivel and die. In short, his analysis of contemporary forms of unbelief sees them as "a crisis of civilization" itself and not purely a "religious crisis."[9]

Velasco's book goes into more detail and usefully distinguishes four types of unbelief. The first consists of rational interpretations of life and takes such various forms as atheism (in the strict sense), agnosticism, skepticism, nihilism and so on. The second type involves subjective responses to religion as perceived—irreligion, indifference, unbelief as distance from the life of church, etc. With the third come some social reactions to religion—for example secularism and anticlericalism. Finally there are forms of unbelief that stress their positive stance rather than the denial of God or faith—"free thinkers," humanists, or rationalists.

Martín Velasco next turns his focus to contemporary unbelief, arguing that this phenomenon has moved from being a stance of some elite thinkers to being now the "dominant cultural discourse." First, there are various kinds of "unbelief inside religion," including "perversions in the institution that incarnates faith" and so-called "civil religion".[10] In this light a certain self-critique by religion is in order. But absence of faith today more often than not is connected with a certain functional horizon and life-style and becomes a form of religious indifference. Insofar as this situation leaves a person closed to any religious questioning, the old "preambles of faith" need now to be interpreted in a more existential manner.[11] This would aim at awakening people from consumerist drifting into some sense of their smothered needs.

As Caffarena also stressed, Velasco notes that a Promethean kind of unbelief is rooted in a certain desperation and anguish, and can be connected with a protest against the tragedies of the world. Developing further than Caffarena, Velasco views the "post-modern" form of unbelief as largely narcissistic, because marked by a retreat into private existence, a passive resignation before history, and a life-style of radical autonomy, sometimes hedonistic and cut off from any authority figures.[12] This complex phenomenon, Velasco argued in Chapter 4, is best interpreted in an interdisciplinary fashion. Thus sociology will offer insights into secularization; psychology can examine the process of disillusion with religion in individual experience; history may analyze typical situations and processes of de-Christianization; philosophy is able to show that there is a wider range of possibilities within reason than the narrowly rationalist; and theology has come to see that just as unbelief is now less intellectual and more practical, so too faith itself is radically existential and never simply a matter of pure epistemology.

In Chapter 5 of his book, Velasco turns from ways of understanding unbelief in itself to a discussion of its converging causes in today's culture. In first place, he puts life-style as often aborting the religious question. After that he offers brief comments on a scientific mentality, on the problem of evil, and on "the scandal of believers," a theme, he adds, that was central in the Old Testament prophets.[13] He also lists a variety of patterns whereby people become alienated from religious practice or belonging. Often these involve a mixture of unanswered rational critiques, impoverished religious formation, and unfruitful church worship. Hence "faith is gradually extinguished due to lack of practice, lack of nourishment, and lack of development of faith."[14]

Modernity and Post-Modernity

As already noted in the reflections of Caffarena and Velasco, there is considerable attention to how the transition to "post-modernity" has altered the tone of unbelief. This topic has been discussed in all language groups, but it seems more dominant in Spanish-language publications. Some more recent authors develop it in different directions, as will now be seen.

Luis González-Carvajal divides his book on ideas and beliefs of people today into two parts, entitled in fact modernity and post-modernity.[15] Under the heading of modernity he studies all the older themes of relevance to unbelief: secularization with its loss of a coherent symbolic universe of meanings, the scientific mentality with its narrowing of truth to one form, liberations of various kinds with their opposition to the church, and the rise of a dominantly middle class culture with its tendency to individualism and consumer life-styles.

The second part of the book explores the emerging and contrasting challenge to faith posed by post-modernity. He insists on the existence of a "post-modernity of the street" as distinct from that associated with various intellectuals such as Lyotard or Vattimo.[16] This means a set of lived attitudes that are very distant from religious faith. It displays various characteristics: an indifference to life-plans and collective hopes; a mixture of hedonism and "self-development"; existence life without moral imperatives; the replacement of *homo sapiens* by *homo sentimentalis,* in other words, rationality by emotivism; the return of various forms of private and experimental religiousness.

Faced with these new challenges to religious belief, González-Carvajal is relatively positive about a pastoral encounter between faith and post-modernity. Such a culture in his view highlights the need to emphasize three dimensions of Christian faith:

(1) initiation into forms of religious experience, a dimension unduly neglected under the pressures of "modernity"; (2) reverence before the mystery of God, and hence a return to negative and narrative forms of theology; (3) renewal of the festive and artistic expressions of Christianity, an aspect forgotten due to the "modern" stress on action.[17]

More recently and in similar style, Antonio Jiménez Ortiz has argued that "practical unbelief" is now the dominant form and one likely to remain so well into the next millennium.[18] His treatment of post-modernity parallels that of González-Carvajal in many respects, and he offers a balance sheet of what is potentially fruitful and potentially dangerous in this new "sensibility." In his view its main characteristics are: fragmentation, sense of difference, pluralism, loss of confidence in progress, rejection of mega-narratives, the end of history, the dominance of the provisional, the ousting of ethics by aesthetics, a revival of nihilism, and (interestingly) humor as self-defense against disillusionment.

He too singles out the need for incarnate experience of faith and for a revival of negative theology. But he adds that the post-modern sensibility invites theology to develop a certain humility, viewing itself as a pilgrim form of meaning, and he insists that against the privatizing tendencies of the post-modern, faith needs to find a new language to challenge the entrenched injustices of our planet. Perhaps that final point suggests that theology of unbelief need not exclude those liberation perspectives with which this chapter began.

Notes

1. Antonio Pérez-Esclarín, *Atheism and Liberation* (Maryknoll: Orbis, 1978), p.58.

2. Ronaldo Muñoz, *The God of Christians* (Maryknoll: Orbis Books, 1991), p.11.

3. Gustavo Gutiérrez, *Theology of Liberation* rev. ed. (Maryknoll: Orbis, 1988), p.128.

4. Gustavo Gutiérrez, "Liberation Theology and Progressivist Theology," in *The Emergent Gospel: Theology from the Underside of History*, ed. Sergio Torres and Virginia Fabella (Maryknoll: Orbis, 1978), p. 241.

5. José Gómes Caffarena, *Raíces Culturales de la increencia* (Santander: Sal Terrae, 1988), p.13.

6. Pp. 31, 34.

7. P. 37.

8. P. 39.

9. P. 41.

10. Juan Martín Velasco, *Increencia y evangelización del diálogo al testimonio* (Santander: Sal Terrae, 1988), pp. 24, 32, 39.

11. P. 41.

12. Pp. 58-61.

13. P. 89.

14. P. 92.

15. Luis González-Carvajal, *Ideas y creencias del hombre actual* (Santander: Sal Terrae, 1991).

16. P. 157.

17. Pp. 186-190.

18. Antonio Jiménez Ortiz, *Por los Caminos de la Increecia: La fe en diálogo* (Madrid: Editorial CCS, 1993), p. 29.

Epilogue

A Unique Experiment

It seems right to end this book with a very brief account of an Italian initiative of dialogue between believers and non-believers. In the course of 1992-1994 Cardinal Carlo Maria Martini published three books of selected interventions from a series of encounters he has promoted annually in his diocese of Milan since 1987.[1] These involved exchanges of high quality between believers and non-believers on different aspects of religious meaning—art, suffering, the role of feeling, the function of intelligence, the nature of the act of faith, the spirit of childhood, the silence of God, Buddhist absence of God, the prayer experiences even of non-believers.

The original name given the series in Italian was "Cattedra dei non credenti," the first word having echoes of both professorial "chair" and episcopal "throne," but the overall intention was clear: to let unbelievers and believers genuinely hear one another. Before an invited audience, the atmosphere was deliberately not one of debate, nor of academic lecture, but rather of reflecting on the roots of faith and unbelief as experiences and as options. As Martini expressed it, introducing the series, the interaction of belief and unbelief can be found within each person and also throughout the Bible, where faith ranges from shy, questing and fragile to struggling and victorious in its trust.[2]

Among the most striking parts of these books are the statements of non-believers, and especially the level of unpolemical honesty that characterizes them. Thus the philosopher Salvatore Natoli links the agonizing experience of Job with that of the centurion at the crucifixion, and ends with this comment: "For me this witness is disturbing. I pay attention to him, but I do not understand. There is another passage of the gospel where it says, 'Nobody can come to me unless I call him' (cf. Jn 6:65). I do not know what this call is, probably because I have not had it. And yet, because it is a mysterious thing, perhaps it has been right to reflect on this problem."[3]

Deeper Than Any Arguments

A similar tone of honest searching is clear in the contribution of the non-believing psychoanalyst Mario Trevi, who spoke of the "waiting" quality of many people before the possibility of an "intuition of transcendence." In his view prayer involves fostering an imaginative or "symbolic space," and as such "prayer" can be present even without faith, provided a person gets in touch with one's essential hunger and finitude. And he adds: "There is no faith that does not contain an element of unbelief and no unbelief that does not contain at least the temptation toward faith.... In a psychological perspective, faith and non-faith not only mix in various proportions, not only alternate, not only give birth to one another, but are complementary."[4] In the same series on prayer, Roberta de Monticelli, poet and philosopher (and non-believer), meditated on the power of poetry to evoke "essential knowledge," "a feeling of the origin," and hence to approach a condition of prayer. She went on to propose that there was a whole wavelength of thinking that had nothing to do with chasing arguments; instead it is a question of "musical thought," rooted in gratitude for existence.[5]

Among the contributions from believers was the personal witness of Enzo Bianchi's account of the darkness of a contemplative vocation: "[The realities of non-belief] teach me that the affirmation of God is not forced, and if therefore I am not compelled to believe, then I am free and my faith is an act of freedom, with nothing at all imposed. But if non-believers exist, there is also a non-believer within me, and I must confess that faith and disbelief live and move within me, that the frontier between them passes through me…. It can be said in a paradoxical way that the believer is an atheist who is unaware of it." [6]

In his reply to this, Massimo Cacciari, as non-believer (as well as philosopher and indeed mayor of Venice), stressed that in the New Testament the grammar associated with the word *pistis*, faith, is quite unusual: it nearly always implies a faithing *toward*, rather than a certainty attained. And in a similarly personal vein, he commented in the understanding of faith, the *intellectus fidei*: "One *must* understand it; even the non-believer must understand it, if he is not to be careless in his exercise of the mind; even the non-believer must understand that true love is found not only (as is held intellectually, abstractly) in the moment of closeness, but in the moment of total separation." [7]

At the Edge of the Ocean

Perhaps Cardinal Martini should have the last word. Reflecting on the surprising depths of communication during the meetings, he asks how one arrives at such a wavelength. This depth is not the fruit of introspection, or of therapy, but of "an authenticity born from the tough and dark moments of life, through which a person arrives, perhaps for the first time… toward the discovery of an inner and powerful feeling, unconquerable, because it surges at last into freedom." [8] And concluding the series of encounters on the prayer of non-believers, Martini develops a metaphor of standing on the shore:

> The human being is faced with an alternative: to close oneself, or reject what one cannot understand or possess, or else to open up in

a different way to this totality, letting oneself be grasped by the inexpressible. To each human being is given the possibility of embracing a capacity for wonder, for reverence, without changing it into something pragmatic—a possibility that is not allowed for in the categorial divisions of faith or non-faith. While grasping or understanding brings us to the brink of an abyss, to the edge of the sea of Being, it is wonder and awe that can spur us to throw ourselves into the waters of that sea. Prayer appears as strength for a further step: allowing us to swim in the sea, and letting us share, if only for a moment, in the understanding of everything."[9]

Notes

1. Carlo Maria Martini, *Cattedra dei non Credenti* (Milan: Rusconi, 1992); *Chi è come te fra i muti?* (Milan: Garanzi, 1993); *La preghiera di chi non crede* (Milan: Arnoldo Mondadori, 1994).

2. *Cattedra*, pp. 13–15.

3. *Cattedra*, pp. 50–51

4. *La preghiera*, pp. 29, 32, 36.

5. *La preghiera*, pp. 54–55, 60.

6. *Chi*, p. 96.

7. *Chi*, p. 109.

8. *Cattedra*, pp. 185–186.

9. *La preghiera*, p. 114.

Select Bibliography

This list is limited to works in English, and includes some works not mentioned in the body of this book. For writings in other languages, the reader is asked to consult the notes at the end of the chapters.

Arts, Herwig. *Faith and Unbelief: Uncertainty and Atheism.* Collegeville: Liturgical Press, 1992.

Buckley, Michael J. "Atheism and Contemplation," *Theological Studies* (XL, 1979), 690-699.

————. *At the Origins of Modern Atheism.* New Haven: Yale University Press, 1987.

————. "Experience and Culture: A Point of Departure for American Atheism," *Theological Studies* (L, 1989), 443-465.

Connolly, John R. *Dimensions of Belief and Unbelief.* Washington, DC: University Press of America, 1980.

De Lubac, Henri. *The Discovery of God.* London: Darton, Longman and Todd, 1960.

————. *The Drama of Atheistic Humanism.* New York: New American Library, 1963.

Fogarty, Philip. *Why Don't They Believe Us?* Dubln: Columba Press, 1993.

Gallagher, M.P. "The Birth of a New Ecumenism: Attitudes to Atheism in Vatican II," *Milltown Studies* (No. 6, 1980), 1-35.

————. *Free to Believe: Ten Steps to Faith.* Chicago: Loyola University Press, 1978.

————. *Struggles of Faith.* Dublin: Columba Press, 1990.

————. *Help My Unbelief.* Chicago: Loyola University Press, 1987.

Gilbert, Alan. *The Making of Post-Christian Britain.* New York: Longman Inc., 1980.

Giussani, Luigi. *The Religion Sense.* San Francisco: Ignatius Press, 1990.

Gutiérrez, Gustavo. *Theology of Liberation.* Revised Edition. Maryknoll: Orbis Books, 1988.

Kasper, Walter. *The God of Jesus Christ.* London: SCM Press, 1984.

Kress, Robert. "Religiously Indifferent or Religious Different," *Kerygma* (XXIV, 1990), 143-159.

Küng, Hans. *Does God Exist?* New York: Doubleday, 1980.

Lacroix, Jean. *The Meaning of Modern Atheism.* Dublin: Gill, 1965.

MacIntyre, Alasdair, and Ricoeur, Paul. *The Religious Significance of Atheism.* New York: Columbia University Press, 1969.

McLelland, Joseph. *Prometheus Rebound: The Irony of Atheism.* Waterloo: Wilfred Laurier University Press, 1988.

Metz, Johann Baptist. "Unbelief as a Theological Problem," *Concilium* (Vol. I, No. 6, 1965), 32-42.

Muñoz, Ronaldo. *The God of Christians*. Maryknoll: Orbis Books, 1991.

Murray, John Courtney. *The Problem of God*. New Haven: Yale University Press, 1964.

Neusch, Marcel. *The Sources of Modern Atheism*. Ramsey: Paulist Press, 1982.

Novak, Michael. *Belief and Unbelief: A Philosophy of Self-Knowledge*. New York: Macmillan, 1965.

Pannenberg, Wolfhart. *Christianity in a Secularized World*. London: SCM Press, 1988.

Pérez-Esclarín, Antonio. *Atheism and Liberation*. Maryknoll: Orbis Books, 1978.

Poupard, Paul. "Dialogue after the Collapse of Communism," *Atheism and Faith* (XXVII, 1992), 81-90.

_____ . *The Church and Culture: Challenge and Confrontation*. St. Louis: Central Bureau, CCVA, 1994.

Priestland, Gerald. *The Case Against God*. London: Collins, 1984.

Pruyser, Paul. *Between Belief and Unbelief*. New York: Harper and Row, 1974.

Rahner, Karl. *Theological Investigations*, 23 volumes. New York: Crossroad, 1961-1992. See especially the following essays: "The Christian among Unbelieving Relations," III, 355-372. "Anonymous Christians," VI, 43-58. "Atheism and Implicit Christianity," IX, 145-164. "Theological Reflections on the Problem of Secularization," X, 318-348. "Theological Considerations on Secularization and Atheism," XI, 166-184. "Experience of Self and Experience of God," XIII, 122-132. "Anonymous and Explicit Faith," XVI, 52-59. "Justifying Faith in an Agnostic World," XXI, 130-136. "The Church and Atheism," XXI, 137-150.

_____ . *Foundations of Christian Faith*. New York: Crossroad, 1978.

Reid, John. *Man Without God: An Introduction to Unbelief.* New York: Corpus 1971.

Six, Jean-Francois. *Is God Endangered by Believers?* Denville: Dimension Books, 1983.

Sölle, Dorothee. *Thinking About God.* Philadelphia: Trinity Press International, 1990.

Sullivan, Francis A. *Salvation Outside the Church?* New York: Paulist Press, 1992.

Turner, James. *Without God, Without Creed: The Origins of Unbelief in America.* Baltimore: Johns Hopkins University Press, 1985.

Tyrrell, Francis M. *Man: Believer and Unbeliever.* New York: Alba House, 1974.

Viladesau, Richard. *The Reason for Our Hope: A Theological Anthropology.* New York: Paulist Press, 1984.

Von Balthasar, Hans Urs. *The God Question and Modern Man.* New York: Seabury Press, 1967.

Walsh, Ann. *Reason To Believe.* Dublin: Veritas Publications, 1994.

Other Books in This Series

Other Books in This Series

What are they saying about Acts?
by Mark Allan Powell
What are they saying about the Ministerial Priesthood?
by Rev. Daniel Donovan
What are they saying about the Social Setting of the New Testament?
by Carolyn Osiek